BSNS & IND

Ready to Work?

Ready to Work?

the development of occupational
skills, attitudes, and behaviors with
mentally retarded persons

David R. Ginglend &
Bernice Wells Carlson

ABINGDON
nashville

READY TO WORK?

Library of Congress Cataloging in Publication Data

GINGLEND, DAVID R
 Ready to work?

 Bibliography: p.
 Includes index.
 1. Mentally handicapped—Employment.   2. Mentally handicapped—
Education. I. Carlson, Bernice Wells, joint author. II. Title.
HV3005.G56   331.5'9   76-58841

ISBN 0-687-35559-1

MANUFACTURED BY THE PARTHENON PRESS AT
NASHVILLE, TENNESSEE, UNITED STATES OF AMERICA

To:

Kenneth F. Glover, principal of Lincoln School, Plainfield, New Jersey,
whose supportive assistance for many years helped to make the training program for severely retarded persons a reality,

and

Dr. Carl Walter Carlson,
whose supportive help made possible the writing of the authors' three books on training severely retarded persons from childhood to adulthood.

Introduction

Here is a book based on sound educational and psychological principles to help prepare mentally retarded persons for the field of work. Although many writers have stressed the interaction between the major developmental areas within the individual, few have been able to translate this principle into concrete educational programming as well as Mr. Ginglend and Mrs. Carlson have done. They recognize that no mentally retarded person is going to be able to hold a job unless he or she is also physically, emotionally, and socially prepared to do so. The authors indicate how activities can be used in promoting growth within these major developmental areas.

During the course of my professional activities, I have had the good fortune of being able to directly observe the first author develop and carry out the training procedures described in *Ready to Work?* on a daily basis over a period of many years. More importantly, I have been able to observe the effects of these procedures on the functioning of a large number of moderately and severely mentally retarded persons while they were still in school and during their postschool years as well. It is with a great deal of satisfaction and pleasure, therefore, that I write the Introduction to this volume by David Ginglend and Bernice Carlson. They have done an outstanding job of providing a clear, easy to follow, and greatly needed guide to programming for the mentally retarded that stems from actual involvement with these young people over an extended period of time.

Writers in the field of mental retardation agree that the goal of achieving some degree of economic efficiency and independence is appropriate and crucial to the full development of all mentally retarded persons. Frequently, however, the task of preparing mentally retarded young people for work begins too late and takes on too narrow a focus. While written primarily for helping retarded persons who have reached their teens, the present volume will also be valuable to teachers and parents of younger retarded children, in that it provides a clear basis for selecting early training activities.

Introduction

The procedures described in *Ready to Work?* indicate that a successful program for mentally retarded persons must be built on a respect for the individual, a recognition that mentally retarded persons have the same basic needs as any other persons, and a conviction that retarded persons are entitled to the same rights and treatment afforded any citizens in our society. The authors suggest that while all persons must be accepted as they are at any given time, growth in knowledge, skills, and attitudes requires that realistic demands be made upon each retarded individual. They also stress the important point that training should occur within a highly organized, reinforcing, and therefore familiar structure that reduces uncertainty about environmental expectations and leads to stability in functioning as a more mature person.

Finally, *Ready to Work?* suggests that training for a job can and should be enjoyable for mentally retarded young people. And it can also be an exciting and rewarding activity for persons who plan and supervise these training activities. *Ready to Work?* does an excellent job of explaining both of these processes and much more. I highly recommend this book for anyone who has the responsibility on a day-to-day basis for guiding the growth and development of mentally retarded persons.

Paul Heintz, Ed.D.
Associate Professor of Educational Psychology
Director, Program in Special Education
School of Education, Health, Nursing, and
Arts Professions
New York University

Acknowledgments

We should like to thank the many people who inspired us to write this book, including class members at Lincoln School and other retarded young people, their relatives and friends. We also appreciate the professional help given by Aseneth Surls and her co-workers at Priviso Area Exceptional Children's Program, Maywood, Illinois, and by members of the staff of Lincoln School, especially Denise Buczek, Dori Knauer, and Laura Anderson, classroom teachers; Winifred MacLachlan, special music teacher; Ann Hulsizer, special art teacher; Marion Kochlein, physical education teacher, Frankie Zurof, special speech teacher; Carolyn Johnson, teacher's aide; and Shirley Howe, school secretary.

Contents

Preface

Great expectations for mentally retarded adults are becoming more realistic all the time. Gone are the days when parents and other advisors were forced to choose between one of two attitudes, despair or false hope, when considering the future of a retarded adolescent.

Today in many communities a retarded adult who is truly ready to work can get a job in a sheltered workshop, a community program, or a private business or industry and keep it. The best of the private and public institutions have viable work programs that offer a retarded person an opportunity to earn something that he can spend for his own luxuries.

Today, the hope—yes, the great expectation—of intelligent parents of a retarded child is that his life shall not be wasted, that as an adult:

He can and will do something useful.

His life will have purpose and meaning.

He will experience some degree of satisfaction in living.

He will work in harmony with other people.

He will earn money and have some say about how he spends it.

Intelligent parents do not care about how *much* money their retarded offspring will earn or what *kind* of honest work he will do. Their concern is that he will be physically and emotionally able to do it. Parents want a retarded adult member of the family to work so that he himself can feel—yes, know—that he is a contributing part of society.

Today's great expectations are in sharp contrast to the actual results of yesterday's training of mentally retarded persons. A survey conducted by the National Association for Retarded Citizens, and answered by 2,804 parents and guardians, produced the following shocking figures:[1]

---

1. The Research Advisory Committee, National Association for Retarded Citizens, *A Survey of NARC Members*, MR Research no. 2 (Arlington, Tex.: NARC Research and Demonstration Institute, September, 1976).

Job Experience for Different Levels of
Mental Retardation Age 21 and Over

	Level of Retardation			
	Profound	Severe	Moderate	Mild
Never held job	94.5	84.4	59.8	34.6
	(52)	(249)	(277)	(71)
Part-time job	3.6	9.2	17.3	22.0
	(2)	(27)	(80)	(45)
Full-time job	1.8	6.4	22.9	43.4
	(1)	(19)	(106)	(89)

NOTE: Parentheses denote number of individuals.

Even with today's improved attitudes toward job training for mentally retarded persons and improved opportunities for employment, great expectations, unfortunately, do not automatically become realities. A retarded adult who tests academically and physically capable of doing a certain job may fail when it comes to day-after-day employment. The frustrating failure may develop because the retarded adult lacks the prior experience in basic skills, the emotional stability, and the ability to sustain activity needed for success in the work situation.

Sometimes a retarded person is actually encouraged to remain a child. His preadolescent activities are continued into adulthood because he is happy doing the things he learned to do as a child. He is not encouraged to learn new skills or to continue doing a job until it is finished.

Being happy is great, but it's not enough for the postschool life of a retarded adult who wants to enter the job market. A person must be ready to work before he can work. Getting ready to work takes training.

Training a retarded adult for fruitful postschool life must start long before the arrival of graduation from a special class program or from a special program in the mainstream of a regular class. Because the retarded person develops skills and grasps academic learning more slowly than his "normal" peers,

Preface

and because each learned skill must be reinforced with frequent repetition, the training of a retarded person for the job market must be carefully planned and systematically executed in the school program.

To successfully plan a job-preparation program for a group of retarded persons in a classroom, a teacher must consider two aspects: (1) training the group as a unit and (2) training each individual, taking into consideration the degree to which his early training, schooling, and life experiences have helped him develop his job potential.

This book takes a hard look at what types of attitudes, social adjustments, and basic skills are needed if a severely retarded adult is to derive any success and personal satisfaction from working. It also gives specific examples of ways to help prepare a group of severely retarded adults for possible job success and success in living as productive and compatible adults.

The authors accept the hard reality that in all likelihood some retarded individuals will not get and hold jobs regardless of their training and their attitudes. There may be conditions in their lives that cannot be overcome. They may, for example, live in rural areas or in communities that offer few if any work opportunities. They may have physical problems, such as frequent seizures; deep-seated emotional problems; or multiple handicaps preventing steady employment. Failure to earn money should never mean failure in life or, for that matter, failure of a training program.

In some cases, being a contributing member of society may mean taking care of one's own needs and at the same time helping—without pay—at home, in a community, or in a residential away-from-home environment. Training and living experiences similar to those described in this book should help a mentally retarded individual find his niche and personal identity in any situation in which he finds himself.

Although this book is addressed largely to teachers, it is for parents too; without the understanding and cooperation of parents or guardians, no job-training program can fully succeed.

Parents must know not only what a special class is doing but also why certain methods are used.

They must know how to be supportive, without interfering.

They must know how to share experiences, so that when the time comes, they can untie psychological apron strings and allow their adult offspring to be as independent as he is able to be, while making sure he still feels secure with family and community connections.

During the past thirty years, the authors have watched a large number of retarded people, including those who are severely handicapped, develop from infants to adults, some of whom have found their places in the working world. They have come to know parents well and have felt free to ask and to expect an honest answer from a question like the following: "What was there in Peggy's training that enabled her to work for money?"

The most frequent answer seems to be, in effect: "No one special thing, but the sum total of a variety of work and social experiences in an atmosphere conducive to growth."

The authors also asked, "Why did Jim stop working?" and the answers were given careful consideration.

During the thirty years the authors have worked with retarded people and their parents, they have had opportunities to observe, analyze, and evaluate a variety of programs, some creative and successful, others of minimum value. They have asked themselves and others, "What kind of training do severely retarded people really need in order to work and live fully?" and then, "How can a training program help to fulfill these needs?"

The lesson plans and class projects described in this book are based on David Ginglend's experience as a teacher in Lincoln School, Plainfield, New Jersey. They involve teaching basic skills and endeavoring to develop well-adjusted, healthy people who can cope with the strains of a job situation. Methods of training individuals for specific jobs are left to directors of sheltered workshops and other job-training programs.

Part I
Learning the Concept of Work and Developing Skills

The first concept that a person in a prevocational training class must grasp is work is work; it is not an activity to be followed as long as a person is interested. A worker must continue to perform a job to the best of his ability until the task is done or until an allotted work period is over. The concept seems axiomatic. Yet many could-be workers fail on the job because the concept has not been instilled.

"I hired that big dumb kid to pile wood for the fireplace," said a man who owns a cottage in northern Michigan. "He's strong enough. He can do it right. But unless I stay right with him, he walks away after he's piled a dozen logs or so."

Blame for this type of failure is placed, far too often, solely on the insensitive employer—or on society in general. Agreed! The world needs more sensitive employers who can bring out the best in retarded workers. But an insensitive employer need not take all the blame for the failure of the retarded person.

A perceptive teacher, parent, or social worker knows that the young man's failure to do the above-mentioned job came about to a large extent because he lacked the prior training needed to hold even a part-time job he was physically and mentally able to do.

The story explains why goals for a job-training program for retarded people must include training in accuracy, endurance, speed, and cooperative and independent functioning.

Trainees in one ongoing program translated these goals in their own words. The rules, written on a large poster, are prominently displayed and read aloud often.

ABOUT WORK	HOW WE WORK
Learn to do it right.	We work alone.
Learn to do it for a long time.	We work with others.
Learn to work faster.	

17

Trainees added other rules picked up from the leader.
If you can't work and talk at the same time, don't talk!
If you can't say something nice, then don't say
anything at all!

Trainees in this group appreciate the importance of the rules
and often keep each other in line. When a fellow worker "goofs
off,", another trainee is likely to say, "You don't know how we
do things here."

"Working right" and "working fast" call for certain basic
skills that require day-by-day development and reinforcement.
Observations of a number of sheltered workshops in the United
States and in foreign countries indicate that the same types of
skills are demanded everywhere.

Finger dexterity, object and symbol discrimination, and
eye-hand coordination are needed in tasks concerned with
sorting, grouping, packaging, and simple assembly. These skills
may be taught and reinforced in a work-period situation,
academic program, and recreational program.

All jobs demand some degree of physical stamina, and many
jobs require a certain amount of lifting and carrying. Any
job-training program must include periods of daily physical
education and recreation that develop and keep in use large
muscles and gross motor coordination.

Work should not be drudgery. A work period should be a
happy time and usually is if the teacher gives the impression
that he, too, likes to work. Some trainees can work and talk. A
few trainees cannot withstand the stimulation of several
activities going on at the same time plus conversation. In all
situations, a successful teacher must use common sense and
sensitivity in interpreting work rules.

Naturally, each trainee must receive a great deal of individual
instruction in a large variety of tasks before he can be placed in
a group work project. A teacher must be sure that a trainee can
do these tasks accurately and with sufficient speed before
placing him on a job that requires the efforts of more than one
person.

The trainee must also learn to do jobs that have more than one step, and to perform them in sequence without constant supervision. And he must learn the meaning of "time break," which is: Work on an assigned job, leave it to do something else, and then come back to the first job and continue working where you left off.

After a trainee has developed accuracy and endurance, he tries gradually to develop speed. He competes against his own record, not the achievement of someone else. He is never permitted to sacrifice accuracy for speed.

One attitude must pervade every aspect of the training program. The trainees are young men and women who must act like adults not children. Each person is responsible for a job that he must do as directed. Retarded adults need not and must not be "forever children" in their own minds or in the minds of other people.

1. Class Management

A smooth-running, cheerful classroom with trainees working together on a job-skill learning project, or with each student working individually according to his own ability, does not evolve by some natural or magic process. Such a classroom is the result of careful planning: long-range planning, month-by-month planning, and day-by-day planning.

Planning includes analysis of basic job skills that must be learned, evaluation of each student's ability, survey of training materials available, consideration of space available, specific selection of equipment, designation of tasks to be done each day and by whom, and much, much more (as the following pages will indicate).

If a teacher is to succeed, he must write out the floor plan of the classroom, write out his lesson plans in detail, write out work sheets, and keep records of the students' progress concientiously. Only when this framework is firmly established can he work freely with his students. He must convey the idea that he knows what must be done, how it must be done, who must do it and when. His organization will help the students learn how to fit into a pattern of planned work. Most mentally retarded young people feel secure when they know what to expect and what is expected of them.

Most trainees will strive to live up to a teacher's expectations if they feel that the teacher not only cares about them but also understands them and expects each one to do his best and act in an acceptable manner. This feeling can come about in only one way: the teacher, because of prior and continued evaluation, really does know each student and understand at what level he can function in doing any given task. Moreover, he has estimated each student's potential and planned for his development through sequential stages of training.

Each student must appreciate the following:

1. The teacher will ask no more of him than he can do.

2. The teacher expects him to work and act like a young adult.
3. The teacher has no favorites. He will praise, scold, or, in an extreme case, expel any student who deserves it.

The teacher has compassion, and so should members of the class. Everyone understands that certain people have specific problems that keep them from "acting as they ought to act." At times there will be a feeling, "We forgive him because we know he's trying to do better."

The firmness and pattern described above does not indicate a need for a rigid classroom situation headed by a dictator. Far from it! A teacher without flexibility, a sense of humor, and a zest for life is lost before he gets started.

Visitors at Lincoln School often remark about the relaxed and cheerful atmosphere and the obvious congenial relationships that exist between trainees and between teacher and trainees. The atmosphere did not just happen. It was developed and worked on. The situation may have looked permissive, but it wasn't. Trainees for the most part had learned self-discipline because they had been disciplined.

Just how to develop discipline in a group so that each member will develop self-discipline will always be an individual procedure. It depends both on the makeup of the group and the personality of the teacher. A teacher, of course, must sometimes approve and sometimes disapprove, sometimes praise and other times criticize the quality of work. It is a good idea to make a point of offering more praise than criticism.

A teacher does not rely solely on words to get his commendation or condemnation across. He also develops communication by example, reactions, gestures, and tone of voice. Long lectures in general terms do little good. In like manner, "gimmicks" for attention and discipline lose their effectiveness when used over and over.

If a teacher is truly displeased, he can let the class know it. There may come a time to really "bawl out" a class. These times should be few, and the class should know exactly why the teacher is angry. Caution: the teacher must realize that this has to be a performance, not a case of allowing himself to develop deep-seated anger that raises his blood pressure. When the class is "in the groove" again, the teacher must continue the program as planned.

It may be necessary, once in a great while, to deny the class an activity that members really enjoy or to cut short an activity because there is general disruption or noncooperation.

A trainee may be removed from a program for a day or so for a very serious infraction of regulations. In this case, trainee, parents, and members of the class must all know that Ken could not come to school because he—(whatever he did). Expulsion should be a last-resort type of discipline.

A wise teacher knows the difference between a serious infraction of rules and unacceptable behavior in the classroom. For example: profanity cannot be permitted, but it is usually stopped when a teacher says sternly: "Look! I know that word. I know you hear that word outside. But I don't like it! Don't use it here! Understand? OK."

Often when a teacher praises a minor achievement of one trainee, another trainee who has no problem in that area may say, "That's easy!"

The teacher's standard answer may be, "Anything is easy when you know how! A long time ago, you couldn't do this. You had to learn how to do it."

The teacher's attitude about himself also helps to bring about the desired relaxed but disciplined atmosphere. If he is willing to say, "I made a boo-boo," trainees realize that no one is perfect. If the teacher does not pretend to be a completely selfless person, trainees may feel, without formalizing their thinking, "He does things for us. Let's do what he wants us to do."

At times they may even bargain with the teacher, who may say: "Look! If I spend my time sweeping up your scraps, I'll be too tired to lead square dancing. I don't care who dropped the scraps. If you want to dance, sweep the floor *now!*"

But bargaining or no bargaining, a wise teacher remains in control of a class. He is the boss and every trainee knows it. The concept that workers must obey the boss carries over from the classroom situation to the job situation.

Prior Planning

"There's a time and place for everything" is a timeworn adage that sets the tone for an orderly classroom workshop. Order not only rescues a work-training program from utter chaos but also gives the retarded trainee a sense of security and purpose.

Although the time schedule for each day in a week will differ and certain work periods may be shortened or lengthened a little when deemed advisable, certain aspects of the time schedule must be adhered to regularly, especially those that involve other people. For example, fixed amounts of time should be allotted for—

1. everyday activities such as opening and closing the school program, going to the lunchroom and leaving it, and, in some schools, going to the gym or playground;
2. special activities held outside the classroom but within the school building, for example, music practice, assemblies, movies;
3. preparation for special lessons in art, music, and physical education;
4. taking a trip or a walk outside the school grounds, with the firm understanding that the group must return promptly at a predetermined time.

Adhering to a time schedule that fits into the plans of other people and other classes can help trainees realize that other people also work on time schedules, and that cooperation makes for friendly association.

Nothing can be more conducive to boredom and disruptive behavior than a group standing around waiting for another group to get ready to do something. It's a great skill to train a group to get ready *on* time but not *ahead* of time. It may be necessary to pressure some slowpokes, or, better yet, to devise ways to make them push themselves. Good planning can minimize the need to do either.

Maximum Use of Space and Choice of Basic Equipment

Maximum use of space and wise choice of basic equipment takes just as much planning as the time schedule. It is a good idea to list the activities that will take place on a more or less regular basis and then draw a room plan indicating where each activity will be conducted, adding a diagram of each piece of needed equipment in its place in the appropriate area. Once you have devised a workable plan, keep it, making a change only when it is obvious that a more efficient arrangement might better serve program advancement.

Certain basic equipment has been found most useful.

1. Sturdy chairs of at least two heights so that trainees of different heights can sit comfortably with feet squarely on the floor.
2. Tall work stools with back rests—to be used at the collating table, the conveyor belt, or during music or other programs if the room has no risers.
3. Trapezoidal tables, because they can be used in a variety of ways. When tables are placed singly, trainees work on solitary projects. When two tables are placed together, six trainees can sit together as a congenial small group for meals, parties, or other events. When tables are placed in one long row or a double row, trainees can sit around them for a general work period.

There must be shelves for containers, tools, paper, pegboards, and other equipment needed to carry on the desired program.

With a general classroom rule of, A place for everything and everything in its place, a trainee who is told to do a certain task knows where to find what he needs without being told over and over again where to look for it. At Lincoln School there was no coddling of any trainee who liked to get attention by asking, "Where's the broom?" (or some other piece of equipment used regularly). The standard response was, "You new here?"

Work Sheets

A job-training program needs work sheets. These work sheets, made out for each trainee, not only help a teacher keep track of and evaluate progress but also give each trainee a feeling of working for a purpose. He is making a record. Also, there is a sense of fairness. A trainee cannot argue, "I did [or did not] do that yesterday." A trainee who reads even a little can look at his work sheet and see a check that indicates he has completed a task in a satisfactory manner. He knows, also, that if there is no check, there was no work.

Work sheets are the teacher's record book. With their help he can evaluate the progress of each individual and compare the work of one trainee with that of other workers in the group.

These work sheets can be kept on a clipboard in alphabetical order for all trainees, or they can be kept in individual trainee folders. The important point is that each sheet give in graphic form the record of each worker. Completed work is checked off each day.

These work records are of great value to a substitute teacher, a supervisor, or anyone else interested in a trainee's record. A work sheet gives a profile of a worker's ability and performance.

Assigning Chores and Positions

Helping trainees develop responsibility, self-control, self-direction, and, in some cases, leadership should be a foremost objective of a pre-job-training program. These qualities do not come naturally; they must be nurtured by giving workers opportunities through which reliability can bud and develop. The teacher must begin where each trainee is, and place him systematically in situations that will help him become less dependent and self-centered and at the same time conscious of his role in a group. The teacher must remember that a trainee cannot be pushed or talked into responsible independence. Too much freedom and too much responsibility too soon may cause a worker to become disoriented. A good teacher, after assigning a task, expects the trainee to work well; at the same time, he remains alert and ready to step in if he senses the trainee is becoming frustrated because the responsibility is too great for him to handle just then.

A good teacher always gives praise and recognition for any performance that a trainee has handled to the best of his ability. He may, however, wish to qualify his praise at times, saying, "We'll do even better next time."

Opportunities for training in responsibility lie not only in designated tasks (such as the ones that follow) but also in any group endeavor. As a group program gets into full swing, a teacher may find it expedient to say often, to certain individuals, "We need you" or "We're counting on you" or "We're depending on you." Each person needs to know he is needed. Only then can he accept responsibility and perform in a self-directed manner within the confines of his assignment.

Rotating Chores

Every worker must be willing to accept responsibilities for the various chores needing daily attention in a classroom. It's a good idea to assign these on a rotating basis and to post corresponding names and jobs in a prominent place. Here are a few.

Lunchroom cleanup. One or two workers may be assigned on a daily or weekly basis the job of wiping off the tables after lunch and checking the floor to make sure that no trash has been dropped in the immediate area. The incentive for doing this job may be the simple question, "Would you like to eat on a messy table?" and the admonition, "We try to leave a place

the way we find it'' (or, in some cases, "better than we find it'').
Once this concept has been instilled, trainees tend to become
careful about not dropping their own trash. They are also quick
to reprimand a careless classmate.

Housekeeper for the day. If a bathroom or kitchen is
attached to the classroom, a housekeeper is assigned to clean
the sinks, throw away paper cups that may have accumulated,
and wash any dishes that were used after the lunch period. The
housekeeper does not put away the dishes but leaves them on
the draining board, or some other assigned place, so that the
teacher can check to make sure that they are really clean and
dry. If the dishes pass inspection, another trainee is asked to put
them away.

The housekeeper may at first need supervision—to be
cautioned perhaps to use only a reasonable amount of
powdered cleanser or spray cleaner, and to wash the entire sink
or washbowl, starting at the top and fixtures, working down to
the bowl, and finishing up by rinsing well so as not to leave
streaks.

Some trainees have learned at home to rinse out a washbowl
after washing paint or dirt from their hands in order to avoid
having a messy washbowl. They have also learned how to
clean a washbowl well. Other trainees need guidance.

Work-period cleanup. One or two workers are assigned daily
to clean up after a work period, disassembling various work
projects and putting parts away in the correct containers. They
may take apart pegboards that have been filled, sort beads by
color and shape, place pegs and beads in the correct
containers, and put pegboards in the assigned storage place. If
members of the work cleanup team have finished their own
work assignments in the morning, they may do part of the
disassembling and sorting before lunch. They may, however,
have to give up part of their free-time period to continue and
finish the job. Occasionally, on very busy days, other workers
may volunteer or be assigned to help them. It is crucial,
however, for every trainee to learn that when a job has to be

done, a worker may be expected to give up some of his free time.

End-of-the-day cleanup. Every class member is expected to help put the room in shipshape condition at the end of the day. What must be done in the way of placing chairs on tables for the purpose of cleaning by the janitor depends, of course, on the school's regulations regarding buildings and grounds. An end-of-the-day cleanup team checks to see that there are no pencils, papers, or other articles on the floor, that windows are closed and shades drawn to the appropriate and uniform height, and that the room in general looks tidy.

Gardener of the week. The job of watering plants in the classroom is usually a coveted one. Most trainees have to learn not to over water plants. The gardener also feeds any pets or fish that the class keeps.

Responsible Positions

Trainees who have shown that they can be trusted to act in a responsible way without constant supervision may be chosen to do special jobs.

Messenger of the day. Most trainees like this job. The messenger for the day takes to the office the attendance slip and lunch order if the class does not do its own cooking. He carries any message or notice that must be delivered to any other part of the building. If the message is at all complicated, the teacher should write it down. Some trainees, however, can deliver short verbal messages correctly if the teacher uses as few words as possible, puts the key words first, and asks the messenger to repeat the words.

Captain of the week. Captain of the week is a post that carries the highest responsibility in the classroom, a job that can be assigned only to trainees who have shown by their performance of other tasks that they have achieved a high degree of self-discipline and dependability. They are people who can handle power without letting power corrupt them. As some trainees working under a captain of the week have phrased the situation, "We're supposed to listen to him, but he shouldn't be bossy." If a captain snaps a dictatorial command in a harsh tone, the teacher may choose to give him a look but make no comment. Often the captain will add "please."

Each captain will handle the job differently; and by careful observation, the teacher can learn much about him.

The teacher chooses the captain of the week on Friday and places the name on a small poster that says "Captain of the Week" in large letters. A permanent sign can be made of oak tag. Slits are made for insertion of a name each week and a pocket attached to hold other names (see diagram next page).

The role of the captain is to get the group in line and lead them in passage to other parts of the building, for example, to and from the lunchroom, to and from playroom or playground, to and from assemblies. He also takes the lead on trips and walks.

The captain has the responsibility for signing all trainees IN at the beginning of the day and OUT at the end of the day. This is done by using sign-in, sign-out boards and slips.

Sign-In, Sign-Out Process

Materials: two pieces of oak tag about twelve inches by thirty-six inches, smaller pieces of oak tag, paper for slips

A class needs two boards: a sign-in and a sign-out board. Cut two pieces of oak tag approximately twelve inches by thirty-six inches. Mark "IN" at the top center of one and "OUT" at the top center of the other. Divide each board into sections large enough to allow you to write the name of each worker, and staple below it a pocket to hold a slip (see diagram next page).

Every Friday, the captain (if he is able to do so) makes out slips for the following week using old slips as models. If he cannot do this, the teacher or someone else prepares the slips. Every slip has a worker's name at the top and two columns below—IN on the left side of the paper and OUT on the right. Under IN and under OUT are five dashes, each representing a working day. For trainees who are advanced in their ability to recognize words, abbreviations for the days of the week may be used. A slip is put in the OUT pocket on the board under each name.

As each trainee arrives at school, he takes his slip from the OUT pocket and hands it to the captain. The captain punches a hole by the dash or name of the day and returns it to the trainee. The trainee then places his slip in the pocket under his name on the IN board. The same process, but in reverse, is followed at the end of the day when slips are transferred to the OUT board.

Trainees who are advanced in printing can sign their names or initials on the slips in the designated place. When they have reached this degree of functioning, the teacher should then make a stencil and mimeograph sign-in, sign-out slips.

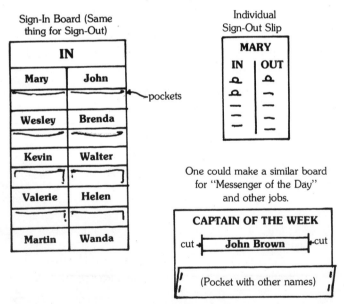

Sign-In Board (Same thing for Sign-Out)

Individual Sign-Out Slip

pockets

One could make a similar board for "Messenger of the Day" and other jobs.

On Fridays the captain for the next week finds his name in the pocket and replaces existing captain's name with his own.

Free-Time Period

Let no one underestimate the value of a free-time period in a job-training program. During this period a trainee shows that he can or cannot function independently as a young adult and behave in a manner acceptable to his community. This is not a stuffy statement, and there is no point in arguing that society should accept every person as he is. Any training program that is to succeed must take into consideration the existing cultural patterns and values deemed "proper" by a population and help young retarded adults fit comfortably into the accepted pattern of social behavior suitable to a particular work situation. Many retarded persons fail on the job because they don't "act right" during coffee-break time, rest breaks, lunch hour, and other free time.

Most social reactions are learned reactions to social situations. A child is taught how to behave when he is in different groups in different places. It would then follow that if acceptable social behavior is taught, unacceptable social behavior can be modified when necessary. Also, acceptable social behavior can be reinforced by repeated opportunities to do things with people. A person can also be taught to do acceptable things by himself.

A word of caution: This free period should not produce an atmosphere of enforced conformity. It should be for each trainee a happy time, a safety valve—a time to release the pressure of structured work, to engage in semi-independent activity, to socialize if he wishes to do so, or to retreat within himself if he feels like it.

Free time in a training program is ostensibly a time when individuals do what they wish to do within the limits determined by what equipment is available in a specified place. In a classroom, for example, working (either alone or with another person) on a large puzzle set on a card table or playing a favorite record would be acceptable activities. Taking a handball out of a pocket and throwing it across the room yelling "Catch!" would not be acceptable behavior in that place. Brushing the puzzle pieces off the table or carrying out any other destructive or unkind act would also not be tolerated—not even as a joke.

During this free-time period the teacher is in the background observing, learning, and stepping in when necessary either to make an encouraging suggestion or comment or to put an end to unacceptable behavior.

What do young adults like to do during this period?

The favorite activity is using the record player, since it cannot be touched at any other time during the day. A number of teen-agers bring their records to school every day. Only designated persons who have demonstrated the ability to operate the player correctly may put the records on the machine. Care is taken, however, to enlarge this privileged group by teaching other class members how the machine operates and guiding them until they can work the machine alone.

Trainees, as a rule, discipline each other about being careful of other people's records, taking turns in choosing what to play, and not pushing around the machine. If certain individuals stir up controversy over the use of their records, or over related matters, they are denied the privilege of bringing records to school until they are mature enough to keep track of their own records and act, in general, like adults.

As a rule, record-playing time is a happy one. A majority of the class members interact verbally, expressing freely what music they like best. Some persons want to listen—often intently—without talking. Others like to dance. A few may imitate TV singers or actors. Others may ignore the music and take part in different activities. The teacher is on hand to offer suggestions.

The teacher may choose to show some pupils how to play simple card games. Or some class members may want to play cards or other table games they have learned at home or in early school training. They may want to continue some handcraft project or do simple embroidery on gifts they are making. Or, they may want to make cards or decorations if a holiday is coming up.

In general, free time is what the name suggests—a chance to do what one wants to do in an informally structured atmosphere but within limits dictated by common sense and consideration of other people.

TV in the Classroom

Something must be said about the use of TV in the classroom either as a free-time activity or as a teaching tool. In the opinion of the authors, its use should be limited to rare occasions of national interest such as the inauguration of a president or an event on a par with the first moon landing—some event that "everyone" will be talking about and from which, therefore, retarded persons should not be excluded.

It must be remembered that in a training program time is precious. There is never enough. Choices have to be made about the use of time. Therefore, it is best to select those activities that promote interaction among people, enrich inner resources, develop skills, and promote physical and emotional growth.

Watching TV is a passive activity that offers little help in achieving the above goals. Moreover, most class members have ample opportunity to watch TV at home, and it is a good idea for them to do so at that time on a limited and selective basis. It is especially beneficial when other teen-agers and adults are viewing programs that may later be discussed.

Educational TV is of little value as a tool in teaching this group of young people, for they must have a curriculum suited to their individual needs. By its very nature, educational TV must be planned for a broad audience.

Moreover, the special programs intended to aid slow learners that have been produced to date are shown not just during school hours but also later in the day. Class members, if they wish, may see the programs at the second showing and profit from them in any way they can. It is folly, however, to sacrifice school time on a regular basis for programs that can be watched at home and that may benefit only one or two persons in the group.

2. Developing Basic Skills and Attitudes

There's a commonality of tasks performed in workshops around the world. For the most part they involve simple assembly and disassembly jobs, sorting and grouping materials, packaging and checking completed work.

If a trainee learns to do the above types of work, following set procedures for a period of time, and if he develops positive attitudes toward work and his fellow workers, he may succeed in a variety of work situations. A teacher, therefore, should help each trainee develop basic skills that can be transferred to learning specific tasks on a job.

A teacher must follow a continuing process of observing and evaluating each student's work performance, discovering his potential strengths and skills, and teaching him to use them to compensate for his disabilities. A program must include continuous practice toward the following ends:

1. Improvement of finger dexterity and manipulative abilities
2. Improvement of visual and tactile discrimination in terms of handling, sorting, and grouping various materials
3. Improvement of eye-hand coordination
4. Improvement of memory in terms of recalling procedure, component parts of a task, instructions, and directions
5. Improvement of physical and mental stamina in terms of working longer periods of time at a given task
6. Improvement of motor and large muscle control in terms of general movement needed for lifting, carrying, stacking, and so on
7. Development and maintenance of highest possible level of intellectual skills

A trainee must learn not only how to do a job but also how to get along in a job situation. A training program, therefore, must help him do the following so that he may succeed in a job situation:

1. Develop pride in work well done
2. Learn to work cooperatively with other people
3. Develop pride in the success of a common project even though this means sublimating his desires to perform a role assigned to someone else
4. Learn to work alone
5. Develop consideration and respect toward others including those either less or more fortunate than he
6. Develop a sense of responsibility
7. Develop self-control
8. Develop an understanding of health and safety rules
9. Improve his communication skills
10. Learn the art of giving as well as receiving in terms of help, kind words, and general consideration

For a number of reasons, a training program based on a concept of providing overall development of the students with provision for teaching general skills is usually superior to a program that is in effect a school-centered model workshop or a program tied directly to a workshop from which it accepts job assignments.

1. Lengthy periods of time (days or even weeks) spent on one task eliminates time for daily presentation of numerous activities that develop other needed skills.
2. Emphasis on one job makes it impossible to meet the broad spectrum of needs of any class.
3. Deadlines and quotas tend to cut into the time needed for social, emotional, intellectual, and physical development.
4. Contracted work for which employees are paid carries the requirement that only workers old enough to get working papers be allowed to participate in the project. But training for work should start as early as the individual is able to profit from the experience—usually

before he has reached the minimum chronological age set by law for working for pay.

5. With a group of students at various levels of development and therefore with various degrees of ability to do a job well, there arises the problem of who should be paid how much for a job.

6. Most important, perhaps, is a feeling that certain periods in life bring changes. During the years in school, a trainee learns how to work on a job. He knows that when he finishes school and gets a job, *working* on a job will not be the same as *learning* to work on a job. In other words, entering a workshop or job situation is a step forward in life, not a repetition of what he has been doing for years.

7. Workshops and on-the-job training programs have their own systems and procedures. Sometimes directors resent what they consider to be competition from a school training program.

This does not imply in any way that there should be a sharp division between a local workshop and school job-training program. The more cooperation and the better the attempt at understanding between directors of somewhat similar but not identical programs, the more effective each program will be.

A teacher may wish to have his class use materials from a sheltered workshop or take a job assignment now and then for actual training. A class should visit a local workshop so that members may learn what the future may hold for them. In some cases a student may work part time at a workshop and continue part time in school if this seems to be in the best interests of all concerned. Cooperation, common sense, and consideration are always more effective than competition between two groups trying to help the same kind of people.

One characteristic most frequently listed concerning mental retardation is the inability of a retarded person to exhibit transfer of learning; that is, to use something learned and apply it to a new situation. It is true that most retarded persons are fearful of using initiative or making decisions in a new situation. A new worker needs to be shown what to do. He needs to be told exactly what is expected of him.

However, once he understands the situation, he will put his learned skills to a new use. For example, a trainee who has learned to put sticks and pencils through slotted cards quickly learns on the job to put hair rollers, pens, rulers, or other items into slotted cards. The trainee who has learned to put together nuts and bolts or to put screw lids on containers will quickly learn to assemble other specific items. The trainee who has learned to sort and group materials can learn to sort and group completely new materials, or to separate materials in a large carton. A trainee who has learned to put a specific number of things into containers quickly learns to put a specified number of other things into boxes or bottles. A trainee who has learned to follow a pattern of assembling pegs and beads can learn quickly to follow directions for assembling a novelty.

Acceptable social behavior that has become a habit and healthy attitudes toward work and people transfer to new situations.

The case history of Randy, a physically well-built but severely mentally retarded young adult, will illustrate the theory of successful transference of learned skills and attitudes from a classroom situation to a job.

When Randy's parents helped him apply for a job that required sorting laundry and putting it in specified places at a local hospital, they stated that he had had special training and gave as a reference the name of the teacher.

The teacher, wanting to be objective and honest with the hospital, wrote that Randy was a mentally retarded young man with a stable disposition, and added that the hospital could gain a dependable, cheerful worker if it would do the following:

1. Patiently show Randy the routine he had to follow
2. Demonstrate the tasks he had to perform
3. Not expect Randy to make decisions or use initiative

The hospital followed the teacher's suggestions. At the time of writing, Randy is completing his sixth year of work at the hospital, has had several raises in pay, is liked by everyone, and is seldom absent from work. The hospital has a good worker, and Randy has a steady job because he had been trained in the basic skills needed for the job, and because he has developed acceptable attitudes toward work and people.

Sorting and Matching

Skill in sorting is needed for many workshop and industrial jobs. It makes little difference what a trainee sorts as long as he gains experience in bringing together identical or similar materials in a specified manner. As he sorts, he uses visual, tactile, and cerebral clues. Even a person with limited intelligence potential can be highly trained if a program starts with a simple activity and proceeds in logical sequence toward an ever-broadening range of activities at every level of competence.

The ability to separate and then match is directly related to development of reading skills as well as skill in observation and memory. A retarded person who scores very low in ability to read for meaning may be able to read names well enough to sort laundry. A so-called illiterate person may be able to read names of streets and buildings and numbers on buses and houses and thus find his way around his neighborhood or travel by public transportation to other parts of the city.

Accumulating Basic Materials

In collecting material for sorting, keep in mind two factors.
1. Easy access of materials for distribution to trainees
2. Amount of storage space
Determine what skills are to be taught, and then make a list of materials that can be used. Although needed materials are not available through educational supply catalogs, they can usually be obtained from friends, parents of trainees, co-

workers, stores, industry in the community, and other sources. A surprising amount of scrap material is very useful; for example, beads, buttons, washers, curtain rings, nuts, bolts, dried beans of various kinds, broken sets of tinker toys or blocks, nails, paper clips, and hooks and fasteners. Avoid objects with sharp edges.

A TV factory donated to Lincoln School classes floor sweepings that contained thousands of different kinds of washers, setscrews, and nuts. A watch factory donated boxes of watch parts, including stems, wheels, and winding caps.

Boxes, cans, and other containers are needed to hold material to be sorted at specific sessions. These containers should be labeled: "Large" (meaning easy for beginners to pick up), "Medium" (of medium difficulty), "Small" (difficult), and "Extra Fine" (most difficult). They should also be numbered as a coding device for record keeping.

Every worker needs a cafeteria tray on which to place his work. He also needs something to hold the materials he has sorted; for example, bowls or other small containers or a plastic box with sections—the kind used to hold knives, forks, and spoons in a drawer.

Sorting and Matching Projects

The first sorting exercise that a trainee tries should be simple enough to ensure success. Projects may increase in difficulty in more or less the following order.

1. *Identical objects.* Give a trainee a can containing two kinds of objects; for example, paper clips of identical size and two-prong brass-headed clips of identical size. The trainee is told to put the paper clips in one can and the two-prong clips in another. At a later date the trainee may be given a can containing three, four, or more objects, to be sorted into kinds of objects.

2. *The same kind of objects of different sizes.* The trainee is given one kind of object in assorted sizes—for example, various

sizes of paper clips—and told to put those that are exactly alike together in various bowls.

3. *The same kind of objects of different colors.* The trainee is given one type of object that comes in different colors—perhaps a variety of buttons. He is told to sort them according to color. At first there may be only two colors. At a later date he may be given a variety of colors.

4. *The same type of objects of varying shapes.* The trainee is given, for example, a can containing beads—some round, some square, some cylindrical. He is told to put round beads into one can, square beads into another, cylindrical beads into a third.

For a beginner, place three, four, or five mixed items in a container. Place ten or more items in a container for an advanced worker.

As work continues, a teacher may want to give trainees smaller and smaller objects to handle, thus improving finger dexterity. He will find means to combine materials in various ways to give new experiences in sorting and matching.

Grouping

Grouping is a logical skill to learn after matching and sorting. It involves placing together parts that will be used in one unit; for example, a rod bracket needs two screws.

At first the trainee is given brackets and screws that fit into the holes. He is told to put into little bags one bracket and two screws. Later he may be told to select only screws that fit into the holes.

A trainee may also be told to put three or more toys into one bag; for example, one ball, one whistle, and one top. Or one ball and five jacks may be packaged together. Another alternative is to have some of the pieces obtained from industry grouped together in a logical fashion.

As a trainee becomes more and more proficient in sorting and grouping, he is usually able to work for longer periods of time. He should be required to do so.

In all of the above programs, a teacher checks each project when it is completed. He may see at a glance that something is wrong. Rather than point out the error, he may say, "I think something is missing here. What is it?" or "I think something is out of place. What is it?" He gives the trainee a chance to discover and correct his own error whenever possible.

Work is always recorded on a work sheet (see p. 150).

After the check-off, a different trainee puts pieces of work into the original containers. The teacher checks his progress, saying, if necessary, "I see something in here that doesn't belong. What is it?"

Assembling Nuts, Bolts, and Washers

Equipment: steel nuts; bolts and washers of various sizes; containers, such as coffee cans and boxes, bowls or additional cans; metal cafeteria tray for each worker.

Steel nuts and bolts may be the most valuable and frequently used equipment in a successful job-training program. First of all, they make sense to a retarded trainee. He can feel as well as see that he is doing something right or wrong. As a rule, his prior experience assures him that nuts and bolts are part of a workaday world.

From a training point of view, working with nuts and bolts develops small muscles, finger dexterity, and eye-hand coordination. Projects using nuts and bolts can range from very simple activities to more complex tasks.

In setting up this job-training program, obtain a large number of nuts and bolts of various diameters and lengths with matching washers. Place them in containers that are numbered and also labeled for identification. A numbered can may hold any of the following:

Nuts and Bolts (one size)

Nuts, Bolts, and Washers (one size)

Nuts, Bolts, and Washers, Spare Parts (mixed sizes)

At the start of each work session, give each trainee a metal tray. (A cafeteria tray is excellent.) Place the nuts and bolts he will use on this tray. The small edge confines units to a specified work space. Ask a trainee to place a piece of paper with his name on it on the tray. If he is asked to leave a half-finished job, he should put the tray in an assigned location. The signed paper will help him and his teacher identify the work.

The trainee must first learn to assemble a nut and bolt, then to assemble bolt, washer, and nut, in that order. When this skill has been mastered, the trainee is asked to make choices. Two different sizes of nuts, bolts, and washers are placed on his tray. The trainee matches a bolt, washer, and nut; assembles the unit; and places it in an empty bowl or can.

He assembles another unit and then checks to see if it is the same size as the first unit. If it is, he puts the similar units together. If the second unit is larger or smaller than the first, he puts the second unit in a second bowl. When he has finished his task, all the assembled bolts, washers, and nuts in each bowl should be the same size. The teacher checks and records progress.

As skill develops, a trainee will be given three, four, or more sizes of bolts, washers, and nuts to assemble, sort, and place in bowls or cans according to size.

In the beginning, the average trainee makes his selection of matching bolt, washer, and nut by trial and error. He learns gradually to use his eyes to determine which parts will fit into a unit. In this project he is constantly using small finger muscles and developing finger dexterity, and at the same time developing visual discrimination in selecting the correct bolt, washer, and nut for one unit.

When a trainee has developed dexterity and accuracy, his work period is extended so that he will adapt to working still longer at a given task. Extension of attention span is an ever-present goal in job training.

Nuts, bolts, and washers must be disassembled and returned to correct containers, ready for another worker to use. This job is given to another trainee to do at a specified time—either right then or the next day. It must be done before closing time on Friday.

Working with Boltboards

Equipment: material mentioned on foregoing project and, in addition, brass as well as steel bolts, washers, and nuts; boards ranging from 6" X 10" to 12" X 24" or larger; vise, brace, and bits the size of bolts; sandpaper; screwdriver; pliers.

After a trainee has obtained efficiency in assembling bolts, washers, and nuts into units, he is ready to work on a boltboard. It is possible to buy boltboards used in testing; but they are expensive and seldom accommodate more than twenty bolts. Moreover, trainees can help in the construction of boltboards, thus gaining experience using tools and sandpaper.

To make a boltboard, rule a board, mentioned above, into quadrants of 1" or ½". At each intersection of lines, make a large pencil dot. Place the board in a vise, with another board beneath to protect the bit. Select a bit and bolt of the same size. (After a hole has been drilled, the bolt will fit into it.)

Allow a trainee to drill the hole. Make sure that he holds the bit straight while drilling. Choose another trainee to drill the next hole. Make sure that each trainee has a turn to drill a number of holes. Continue the construction of the boltboard until there is a hole at every pencil dot.

When all the holes have been drilled, complete the project by having trainees smooth the edges with sandpaper. This gives the trainees additional exercise and experience with equipment and also produces a boltboard with no scratchy edges.

Put into a container the bolts, nuts, and washer to be used while working on one board. Write identical numbers on the board and container.

A trainee working on this type of boltboard progresses in the following steps (each step representing a start-to-finish procedure):

1. Fills each hole with a bolt on one side, nut on the other.
2. Fills each hole, as above, making sure that the heads of all bolts are on one side of board.
3. Places a washer on a bolt before inserting it into the board.
4. Uses a double washer, one on the bolt before inserting it into the hole, another on the bolt before attaching the nut on the bottom of the board.

The teacher may want to complicate any of the above steps by having the trainee use both steel and brass bolts, nuts and washers, inserting them into the boltboard in a particular pattern such as alternate rows of each kind or a concentric border.

After a boltboard has been assembled and checked, it is given to another trainee for dismantling. If bolts are tight, a trainee can use a screwdriver and pliers to loosen them, thus gaining additional practice in use of tools. This trainee places nuts, bolts, and washers in the correct container, making sure that the number on the container and the number on the boltboard just dismantled are the same.

Advanced Boltboards

Make boards that will accommodate bolts of different sizes. Mark a board into quadrants as in the previous project. Select appropriate bits: ¼″, ⅜″, ½″, ⅝″, ¾″, and so on. Decide on a pattern to be drilled on the board; for example, alternating sizes in one row, alternating rows with all holes in one row the same size but the following row a different size, or any other pattern. A class should eventually have a number of boards ranging from simple to complex. Lincoln School class had forty of them.

Before starting work on a complicated board, the trainee dumps onto a cafeteria tray nuts, bolts, and washers from a can numbered for that board. If he finds that he lacks sufficient nuts, bolts, or washers to complete the board, he goes to the section where the container marked "Spare Parts" is placed and selects the item he needs.

When the board is later disassembled, the container should then hold the exact number of parts needed for the assignment.

Working with Paper

A number of jobs in sheltered workshops and businesses involve working with paper and paper products. Basic skills must be learned; but once mastered, they are usually retained. There is no need for frequent practice, as with nuts and bolts.

If trainees learn how to work with paper and then have a chance to use the basic skills once a month, they will quickly fall into the groove of an assigned operation.

The office wastebasket is the best source of supply of used but unfolded paper such as mimeographed tests and overruns of reports. Schools vary in the amount of paper they may accumulate in this way. If a teacher needs additional used paper, he may be able to get some from other schools, from business firms, or from a college professor who gives tests and requires that the mimeographed sheets be returned.

Folding Paper

Materials: new large and small envelopes with windows, regulation size; quantities of used but unfolded typing paper; cardboard.

Letters written on regulation-size typing paper are folded in one of two ways before they are fitted into large or small envelopes of regulation size: they are either folded into thirds, or in half and then in thirds.

Give each trainee a piece of cardboard that will fit into a large envelope. The trainee proceeds to fold the paper in the following steps:

1. Places cardboard on bottom of paper.
2. Folds paper over cardboard.
3. Creases paper.

4. Removes cardboard.
5. Folds over double portion of paper.
6. Creases folds.

To fold paper for insertion into smaller regulation-size envelopes, give each trainee a piece of cardboard that will fit into the envelope. The trainee proceeds in the following steps:

1. Folds paper in half, with the top and bottom together, making sure that the edges are even.
2. Creases fold.
3. Places the cardboard on the side of the paper.
4. Folds paper over cardboard.
5. Creases paper.
6. Removes cardboard.
7. Folds over remaining paper.
8. Creases folds.

Some trainees will soon be able to fold paper without the cardboard pattern. Others may not master the skill easily.

The next step is to stamp these letters with a name and address in order to prepare them for stuffing into envelopes. This procedure gives the trainees two types of experiences.

1. He learns to use a stamp, making sure that the letters are right side up and the name and address is placed neatly in a correct place.
2. Later, in stuffing the envelopes, he must check to make sure that the name and address show through the window. In other words, he must insert a letter right side up and right side front.

To make a pattern for stamping, remove the back and window of envelopes of each size. In the stamping project, the trainee places the pattern over the folded paper and stamps the name and address in the center of the opening.

Envelope-Stuffing

Materials: regulation-size large and small envelopes with windows, folded letter, rubber bands, additional sheets of paper cut the size of flyers

A trainee is given a pile of folded letters and told to put a letter in each envelope and to place the stuffed envelopes in piles with window side down.

When he has mastered this skill, he is given folded letters, the same number of additional sheets of paper (to represent flyers), and envelopes, and told to place a letter and a flyer in each envelope.

When the envelopes have been stuffed, that trainee, or another, is assigned to sort the envelopes into piles of five, making sure that all of the addresses are on top, and putting a rubber band around each bundle. The number of letters in each bundle can be increased to ten at a later date.

The finished job is placed with other completed work, to be disassembled at a later time.

Skill in paper-folding and envelope-stuffing may give trainees a real chance to serve their community. Several trainees may belong to recreation groups sponsored by the local chapter of the National Association for Retarded Citizens, Easter Seal, or other organizations. At fund-raising time, trainees may take on a class project of stuffing envelopes for mailing. This project can be done during a work period.

A word of caution: A teacher must be careful not to commit the class to doing so much work of this type that other aspects of the training program are neglected.

Cutting Paper

Materials: paper cutter, quantity of paper, rubber bands.

Scrap paper, cut into appropriate sizes, is useful for a number of purposes. Trainees at Lincoln School supplied office workers and teachers with packs of scrap notepaper, and the class used quantities for their own work orders and sign-in, sign-out slips (see p. 30).

Needless to say, a paper cutter is a potentially dangerous instrument if care is not taken in its use. Each trainee should be given a chance to use a paper cutter, but a teacher must give careful instructions and maintain close supervision in the beginning. Then a teacher must use great discretion in deciding which trainees can use a paper cutter independently. Only a few selected trainees will eventually be able to cut paper independently.

Quartered sheets of typing paper are ideal for scrap notepaper and for class work-orders. To prepare a pack, a trainee follows this procedure:

1. Picks up four pieces of paper, making sure that the edges are even.
2. Folds the four pieces of paper at one time, making sure that edges are even.
3. Creases the fold.
4. Opens the paper.
5. Using a paper cutter, cuts the paper in half along the fold.
6. Folds the half-sheets of paper in half, and follows the above steps to produce quarter sheets of paper.
7. Places quartered sheets of paper in a pile, and continues to quarter sheets of paper until the pile is a usable size.
8. Puts a rubber band around the pile.

To produce smaller sign-in, sign-out slips, cut the paper as above and then cut the quartered paper once more, making slips the size of one-eighth of a sheet of paper.

Collating Paper

Materials: folding collating table or collating area, collating racks, assorted paper, paper clips.

Collating, for the purpose of this book, refers to the act of assembling pieces of paper in a designated order.

Every classroom should have a folding collating table or a built-in collating area. The best type of table is one that can be raised or lowered in height because of slots and clamps in the legs. If a trainee is to work standing, he needs a table higher than a card table. If he is to sit, he needs a surface that is card table height.

A collating area is a shelf thirty to thirty-six inches wide, and the correct height for working while standing. It should have two shelves above it ten to twelve inches deep, and below it, twenty to twenty-four-inch-wide shelves as far down as the floor. When this space is not being used for collating, it can be used as a place to put completed or uncompleted work, painted objects while they are drying, and so forth.

Obtain an assortment of different kinds of flat paper that is clearly distinguishable by color or size. On a rack above the collating area, pile similar amounts of each type of paper in the order to be collated.

The trainee proceeds in the following manner:
1. Takes a sheet of paper from the first pile. Places it on the table or wide shelf, face down.
2. Takes a sheet of paper from the second pile. Places it face down on top of the first sheet of paper.
3. Continues to take a sheet of paper from each pile, placing it face down on the other papers. The papers are now in a pile in the correct order for distribution.
4. Fastens the pile of paper together with a paper clip.

A paper clip is used for class practice for two reasons: (1) some trainees have trouble using a paper clip, and the work gives them needed exercise in finger dexterity and eye-hand coordination; (2) it is easier to disassemble papers held by a paper clip than it is those held with a staple.

The collated papers can then be counted into groups of five or ten (like the stuffed envelopes) and held together with rubber bands.

For a different project, a trainee collates a certain number of papers plus a flyer. It is fairly easy for a teacher to collect a number of flyers, which need not match for this practice.

For an advanced project, a trainee collates papers that look similar but are numbered in sequential order. For this exercise, he must concentrate on taking page one, page two, page three, and so on. He has no color- or size-of-paper clues to tell him he is doing the job right or wrong.

When trainees have developed the skill of collating, they may do actual work for the school or an organization. Trainees at Lincoln School did the collating for the office. Here they learned an additional skill—stapling in exactly the right place.

Stapling is required in many workshop assignments and business jobs, including pricing merchandise. It is a skill well learned.

Assembling Cardboard Dividers

Materials: cardboard dividers.

A variety of food preserved in glass jars is packed in cartons that have cardboard dividers separating them from each other. In some stores, workers put stock on shelves and then place long dividers in one carton and short dividers in another to facilitate disposal. A teacher may be able to obtain cartons filled with folded dividers. A large number of dividers can be stored in two cartons.

Putting dividers together is a job still done by hand in many workshops. Trainees seem to enjoy putting them together because in a short time one person can assemble a "mountain high" project. Anyone can see that he's been working!

When dividers have been put together correctly, the teacher checks the work, marks the trainee's work sheet, and assigns another worker to take the dividers apart and put them in the correct cartons for storage.

Individual Assembly Assignments

A trainee who hopes to enter the job market must learn to work at a repetitive job for a considerable period of time without stopping. He therefore needs job-related assignments that he is expected to work on for at least half an hour at a time.

Once a trainee has learned to do this type of assembly work by himself, he can also do it on an assembly line.

Filling Containers

Materials: transparent plastic pill bottles, material to be placed in bottles.

Many workshop assignments involve, in essence, placing a specific number of a variety of objects into a plastic pill bottle and capping it, or putting objects into other types of containers. Any list of useful small materials would be too long to print here. An alert teacher is always adding to his collection in order to give the trainees the experience of identifying and handling a variety of objects of different shapes and sizes. It is one experience to pick up a fat nut and put it into a bottle. It's another experience to pick up a small-sized shirt button and put it into the container. Changing materials to be used amounts to changing assignments, and takes away part of the boredom of doing the same thing in the classroom time after time.

Accuracy and undivided attention to work are the goals of the assignment. Because this work is done on an individual basis, assignments are given in accordance with the ability of each trainee.

The teacher gives the trainee a box of transparent pill bottles and tells him to place specific things in each bottle (for example, one button and two screws) and then to cap the bottle. When the trainee has filled all the bottles as directed, the teacher can spot-check the work at a glance.

Similar tasks can be done using envelopes as containers. A teacher must empty contents of the envelopes into his hand to check for accuracy.

Sticks on Cards

Materials: slotted cards, tongue depressors, or pencils.

A common job in workshops is attaching objects to cards by fitting the objects into slots on the cards. Ball-point pens, pencils, screwdrivers, and other objects are often packaged for sale in this way.

Make a box of cards by cutting oak tag paper approximately

2″ X 6″ in size. With a chisel ¾″ to 1″ wide, hammer two or three slots through a number of cards at a time (see sketch for sample).

A worker receives a box of cards, a box of tongue depressors or pencils, and a box marked "Finished Work." He places a tongue depressor through the slots and places the card in the "finished work" box. He continues to work until all of the objects are on cards.

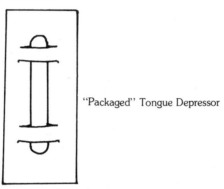

"Packaged" Tongue Depressor

Assembly-line Projects

Many jobs are done in assembly-line fashion. Needed skills and principles can be taught in a classroom through a variety of projects that involve putting an assortment of objects into a container that is passed from trainee to trainee. It is desirable to include this type of training in each week's work plan.

A group can simply work at a table, with trainees passing the container by hand from person to person; but if a group can work with objects moving on a conveyor belt, members will gain added job skills. Some of the advantages of using a conveyor belt are:

1. It is directly related to many "real life" jobs.
2. It provides a task in which all trainees work in close proximity to each other.
3. It accentuates the dimension of timing. The container on

the belt moves along whether the trainee has completed his task or not. A trainee must learn to cope with a low-grade type of tension produced by the realization that a task must be done in a limited time.

4. It is a good medium for developing and gauging speed of productivity for many trainees.
5. It quickly reveals the distribution of abilities within the group.
6. It seems to fascinate all trainees as well as visitors.
7. It represents a different and distinctive work area in the classroom.

The conveyor belt used at Lincoln School was eight feet long, had a speed control from very slow to fast, and was safe in every way. The school attached wooden shelves to both sides to provide space on which to put materials being packaged. The machine was placed a sufficient distance from the wall to allow trainees to stand or sit on both sides of it.

A friend of retarded people donated the conveyor belt used at Lincoln School. A diligent search in any community may produce a similar friend who is able to locate a simple conveyor belt and who can persuade the owner to donate it to a training class.

All trainees can work on a conveyor-belt project, but not in every position. There are stress points. For example, if the trainee placing the containers on the belt is slow, other workers are standing about with little to do—hardly a challenging situation. If the starter works too fast, bottlenecks can develop along the line. If the packer working at the end of the belt is slow and unable to keep up, the arriving containers create a bottleneck.

The important task of the teacher is to assign each job in terms of the ability and speed of the trainee. In other words, simple tasks for the less able, more complex tasks for the more able.

A beginning trainee may be asked to pick up only one item and put it in the moving container. The important idea is to make it possible for him to be a part of the group job and to experience success while working there. More able trainees are assigned tasks of sufficient difficulty to tax their abilities.

The teacher must also plan the tasks in a way that will result in a fairly even flow of work along the line. For example, if the trainee placing containers on the belt is a fast worker, he may be required to place materials in the container before he puts it on the belt. If the trainee at the head of the line is a slow worker, he may be told to take a box, remove the lid, and place the container on the belt.

Another important task for the teacher is to see that the jobs and materials vary as much as possible, so that each trainee will have the opportunity to do as many different tasks as possible in the course of the program. The variety of tasks is limited only by the kind of containers and materials available.

Needless to say, this type of group activity requires a lot of planning that must be done before the class. This may be a good place to state an often overlooked truism: Busy workers are usually happy workers. Idle workers, on the other hand, lose interest in a project to be presented, and often take part in unacceptable activities quickly. The greatest obstacle to the success of any program is to have trainees sitting around doing nothing while the teacher scrambles to get materials together for the next activity. A work period is a work period; and a leisure period is some other specifically designated time. Trainees must be able to work when it is time to work.

After a teacher has made his plans, he writes out work orders. He puts containers to be used in a large carton, and places the carton at the head of the assembly line. He also puts materials to be packed at the places where the trainees will sit or stand. He then puts an empty carton for holding packaged products at the end of the line.

As a rule, the entire class works on a group job. The teacher gives out work orders and makes sure that each trainee understands what he is expected to do.

This can be done the day before the group works on the

assembly line. While the trainees are working on individual projects, the teacher may call each worker to the assembly belt and say, for example, "Jean, tomorrow we are going to work on an assembly-line project. Your job will be to stamp a piece of paper. Put the paper on the belt." The teacher then puts the pile of papers and the stamp on the shelf at the point where Jean will be standing and shows her in advance a sample of what she will be expected to do.

On the work day, the teacher assigns each worker to his work spot and repeats the instructions. Then he files his work orders for the day on a spindle, so that he can easily assign a somewhat different task to each worker for the next project.

The following sample assignment for a day illustrates the variety of tasks a group with mixed abilities might perform while working on an assembly line with a conveyor belt.

JOHN: Assemble containers and place two pieces of folded paper in bottom of each before placing it on the belt.

MARY: Place one button, one washer, and one tile in a small envelope.

SUSAN: Fill plastic pill bottle with dried beans and cap it.

WALTER: Place tongue depressor on slotted card.

JIM: Assemble one brass and one steel nut, bolt and washer.

MILDRED: Place one each of yellow, red, and blue tubing in container.

KEN: Assemble small nut and bolt, place in small box, and close container.

HARRY: Assemble electric coupling (five parts).

LOUISE: Place one pencil in container.

JEAN: Stamp a slip of paper.

BRENDA: Packer—check contents, close container, secure with rubber band, pack in box.

One way to check containers is to weigh them. This method is sometimes used in workshops. For example: A group is hired to fill Christmas stockings with a variety of toys. Each stocking is weighed as it comes off the line. A wrong combination of toys would change the weight.

When convinced that trainees are working with a reasonable degree of accuracy, the teacher does spot-checking on the finished work. If a group does not finish a job on the day it is begun, the project may be carried over to the next day. Work completed in one period is placed in a specified holding area.

At the completion of the job, all filled containers and all leftover materials are placed together. At a later time, two or more trainees are assigned the task of dismantling the job. The best procedure is to empty material in all the containers into a large carton, to put the containers away, and then take apart materials and sort them.

Break Time

If a job is of long duration, it is important to establish the idea of break time. The teacher sets an oven timer for five minutes. The ringing bell is a signal for "Back to work."

The teacher should take note of what trainees do during this break time without dictating what should be done. Break time is similar to free time. Use of free time indicates something about a person's total personality.

Some trainees will take a drink and socialize. Others may return to their regular places and continue with seatwork started earlier in the day. Still others may continue to assemble materials for their task at the belt in order to have a supply on hand when containers pass before them. This could be a sign of feeling insecure with the job or of a desire to give a superior performance. Or, it could mean nothing at all.

Extension of Skills to Community Service

A teacher may find ways to have his class practice assembly-line skills and at the same time perform a community service. For example, each year the Plainfield, New Jersey, Chamber of Commerce sponsors a dinner for new teachers in the school system and presents each teacher with a shopping bag filled with products from local stores and industries. In earlier years, chamber of commerce members filled the bags. The work trainee class at Lincoln School asked for the privilege of performing the task. The job was done assembly-line fashion.

The project had many beneficial side benefits:

1. Trainees felt that they were a useful part of the community.
2. Trainees were intrigued with the different products, talked about them, and in some cases read the labels.
3. Trainees enjoyed the resulting publicity.

Through the publicity, potential employers learned about the training class and what members were learning to do. In talking to employers, the teacher made his wants known and located sources of useful material.

Through the publicity, also, the general public learned something about the practical type of training being done at Lincoln School.

A class may take on a few work orders for pay. However, these jobs should not be so numerous that they crowd out other aspects of the training program. Money earned might well go for a group project such as additional bowling or a picnic. Individuals should look forward to earning money for themselves when they are ready to enter a sheltered workshop or hold down a job on the open market.

3. Developing Kitchen and Sewing Skills

Learning kitchen skills involves more than being taught how to cook in a restaurant, and learning sewing involves more than being taught how to use a commercial machine in a factory or even how to make one's own clothing at home. Chances are that no retarded person will become chef in a large hotel or manager of a custom-made clothing shop; but a number of retarded persons have found employment in the area of food service, and some have worked in jobs related to sewing.

All retarded persons living at home can use any homemaking skills they have learned. A mother of a trainee at Lincoln School said to the teacher, "You will never know how much it means to us that you taught Harry how to make coffee. My husband and I both work. Every morning Harry gets up before we do. He measures the coffee and water just the way you taught him to do and plugs the electric percolator into the socket. When we come downstairs, a pot of coffee is ready and waiting for us."

A severely retarded woman living in a nursing home for the aged was the only resident who checked her clothing when it came back from the laundry each week and sewed up rips by hand. She also did simple embroidery. She had never learned to read; but as a child, she had learned to sew by hand. In fact for many years she sewed pieces of cloth together in intricate designs for patchwork quilts that her mother assembled. Those quilts were never put up for sale; but on today's market they would have brought high prices.

Kitchen Skills

The ability to set a table correctly, wash and dry dishes, and prepare some simple foods will make a retarded person an asset at home and may aid him in being more independent in caring for his own needs. Moreover, he may find employment in some type of food services if he knows how to use certain equipment in the field, has learned to willingly follow directions, is neat, accurate and thorough, and can and will work for an extended period of time.

The scope of training that a teacher can give in the field of food services will, of course, depend upon the setup of the school. Few classes have their own kitchens, and few will be permitted to use school facilities, due to their heavy use for general school purposes. Few school systems provide sufficient staff needed for closely supervised instruction. Any group, however, can learn to set a table correctly and to perform many tasks related to food preparation.

The purpose of training is not to prepare elaborate menus or to duplicate training that class members may be receiving at home. The purpose is to develop general skills that can be used in other situations (or as the basis for on-the-job training) and to ascertain which of the trainees seem to have enough potential in the field to make further exploration and training in a job-oriented program feasible.

Experience at Lincoln School indicated that it is not feasible to try to instruct a large group at once. Training in kitchen skills must be done individually or in groups of three or four. Trainees need direct supervision. It is impossible to keep other trainees meaningfully busy in a kitchen and at the same time give full attention to three or four people.

Members of the Chef's Club at Lincoln School were grouped in pairs, with an able trainee working with a less able one. The remainder of the class worked on routine school assignments while the teacher instructed the "chefs."

In setting up a kitchen-skill program, decide first which skills should be established and make up a work sheet for each trainee (see sample). Record the number of each trainees' experiences in each skill, and with a symbol, evaluate performances in each skill. See the chart on page 61.

In some schools, trainees are able to gain experience in certain areas of food service by helping to prepare and serve food at the school cafeteria on a rotating basis.

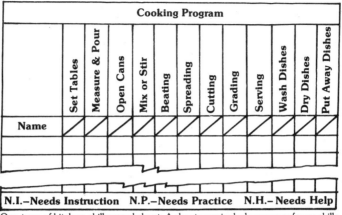

Cooking Program											
	Set Tables	Measure & Pour	Open Cans	Mix or Stir	Beating	Spreading	Cutting	Grading	Serving	Wash Dishes	Dry Dishes	Put Away Dishes
Name												

N.I.–Needs Instruction   N.P.–Needs Practice   N.H.–Needs Help

One type of kitchen-skill record sheet. A sheet may include more or fewer skills than those shown here, depending on the particular program the teacher has designed.

For example, a strong boy who can identify labels (although he cannot read for meaning) is given a list of canned fruits and vegetables needed for the day. He gets these from the storeroom. Or a trainee sets on the counter the silverware and dishes to be used. Or he may do some simple tasks in food preparation. As with workshop assignments, a certain amount of experience is valuable. But no trainee should work so much in the school cafeteria that he loses out on other types of training.

Equipment Hints

1. Avoid the use of open flames. An electric range, or even a hot plate, is safer than a gas stove with a flame.

2. Avoid frying food with grease that may splatter. Most foods that by tradition are fried can also be baked.

3. Use serrated knives. The cutting edge is clearly visible. Accidents are less likely to happen when cutting vegetables and fruits using serrated knives than when using sharp-edged knives.

4. Avoid using a measuring cup with fractions on its side. Use instead a set of cups with a number—¼, ⅓, ½, or 1—pressed into the appropriate cup. To aid a cook in finding

the correct cup, paint the above numbers, about three inches apart, on a shelf. Place the correct cup above each painted number. In selecting the cup to be used, the cook matches the number in the recipe with the number on the shelf and the number on the cup. Many retarded people who cannot understand the concept of fractions can match numbers.

5. Whenever possible, use recipes that avoid fractions in measuring spoonfuls. Packaged products of cakes, cookies, and hot breads require no measuring of dry ingredients. If, however, you wish to use a recipe that has fractions of a spoonful, use various sized spoons that are clearly marked.

6. Make a point of teaching how to read the settings Warm, Low, Medium, and High on an electric range. If the stove does not have these markings, devise some way of marking them on the stove. Adjust recipes to correspond to markings for the heat on the stove.

7. Use a double boiler for cooking such foods as cream sauces, puddings, and hot cereals. The water beneath the food helps avoid burning, sticking, and scorching and also keeps food warm if there is a delay in serving.

8. Teach a trainee to check the handle of a pan each time he sets it on the stove, and make sure that nothing is jutting out over the edge. Many normal people have been badly scalded by bumping into a protruding handle and overturning hot liquid onto themselves.

Teaching Hints

A trainee learns best how to set a table if he has a pattern. The pattern can be drawn (see sample), or a teacher can cut out pictures and paste them in place. The results seem to be the same.

Many retarded persons have a tendency to reverse the setting. They should be required to correct the mistake. They can—and they must—learn to do the job correctly.

Some trainees need the help of counting aids—for example, toothpicks. To illustrate: The standard type of frozen orange juice requires one can of juice and three cans of water. Put three toothpicks on the counter, slightly to the left of where the trainee will stand.

The trainee opens the can and puts the contents into a pitcher. He measures one can of water and puts it in the pitcher. He moves a toothpick from his left side to his right. He continues the process until all the toothpicks are on his right side and the juice is diluted according to directions.

Coffee can be made by the same counting method.

Don't expect a retarded person to read a label. Tell him each time what to do. For example, canned soup is usually diluted with one can of soup and one can of water. Certain varieties of soup now on the markert are not diluted.

If you wish to extend the cooking program and have a practice teacher or other aid to help you, look for simple recipes. A number of tested, easy-to-make dishes appear in *Recreation for Retarded Teenagers and Young Adults* by Bernice Wells Carlson and David R. Ginglend (Abingdon, 1968).

Table Place-Setting

Shown below is the basic place setting that a trainee should learn, with concentration on "left of the plate" and "right of the plate." Once a trainee has mastered the skill of setting a table for one, he can move on to settings for two, three, or four.

He can also learn where to place other dishes to be used for a specific meal, for example, salad bowl or dish, soup bowl, additional silver, and cup and saucer. These dishes are not included in the basic setting because in many families only adults drink tea or coffee, and often these are served toward the end of a meal.

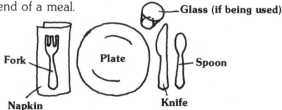

Sewing

Sewing is not likely to play a major role in the school curriculum of severely retarded young people. A teacher may wish to introduce a project of sewing on buttons as seatwork. After the trainees have learned the procedure, he may decide to keep a mixed assortment of buttons, needles, and thread in a convenient place. A class member who discovers that a button is missing on his shirt may sew on a new one if he wishes, or one of his friends can do it for him.

Some class members who have been taught at home to do simple embroidery such as cross-stitch or running stitch may want to bring a small project to school and work on it during the leisure period. A trainee should be encouraged to do so. If other class members show an interest in this kind of work, a teacher can take the cue and fit hand sewing into the program as he sees fit. A situation sometimes develops wherein one retarded teen-ager teaches another how to make simple stitches.

Few schools can afford the equipment and the trained personnel to be able to teach sewing on a home machine on a one-to-one basis as it must be taught. The following method, however, was tested and used while teaching retarded teen-agers in a school that put great emphasis on homemaking skills.

Machine Stitching

The most difficult thing about learning to sew with an electric sewing machine is comprehending how to control the speed of the machine by pressing a lever with the knee or a pedal with the foot and at the same time guide the fabric as it progresses under the needle. A retarded person must approach the learning process step by step.

1. Let the retarded person sit before a sewing machine that has no needle. Have him place his hands on the cabinet in the

center of the machine. Now have him press the lever or pedal, making the machine go very slowly, and then a little faster. Never allow anyone to race a sewing machine.

2. Place a piece of typing paper under the presser foot. Then, still without a needle or thread, teach him to guide the paper under the foot while running the machine. Show him how to hold the paper without getting his fingers too near the foot.

3. When he seems to be at ease in running the machine, put a needle in, but do not thread it. Draw a straight line on paper, and have him practice stitching down the line. Repeat.

4. When he can stitch well on a straight line, draw curved lines and intersecting straight lines on a piece of paper. Show him how to lift the presser foot when he finishes one line and lower it when he starts another.

5. When he has become proficient, draw simple designs on fairly heavy construction paper. Have him stitch without thread along the lines. Hold the paper against a window to let the light shine through the holes.

6. When the trainee has shown that he has mastered the skill of running the sewing machine safely, let him practice sewing straight lines on fabric. Begin as soon as possible to have him sew something he can use or give as a gift.

4. Reinforcing Intellectual Skills

Intellectual skills, as used in this book, mean, in a very narrow sense, academic skills involved in the traditional three Rs—reading, writing, and arithmetic—plus a few related skills such as following patterns while working with pegboards and beads.

Although to the authors' knowledge it has not been established in research, there is strong evidence that teaching mentally retarded children to read and compute is often begun at too early an age and discontinued too soon. Normal children, as a rule, are taught to read when they reach the mental age of six years. Retarded children do not reach this mental age until they are in their teens or preteens. Perhaps this fact explains why many mentally retarded persons seem to have a spurt in learning ability during the second decade of their lives.

This spurt, however, does not occur automatically. A retarded child must have years of experiences in strong readiness programs for reading, number awareness, and use of a pencil if he is to develop his intellectual potential as a young adult.

The years during which a retarded student is being prepared for work are often his final years of formal training. If he is to receive any help in developing his intellect, he must receive it during this phase of his schooling. It is, therefore, of utmost importance for a teacher to assess and evaluate each trainee's achievements and capabilities and then try to help him develop his intellectual potential as far as possible.

We are not suggesting here that the training program become heavily academic. Too many retarded teen-agers sit out their final years of school in watered-down imitations of a traditional school program. The authors are urging teachers to do everything humanly possible to help each trainee improve his ability to handle money, write his name and other words, and develop a usable "sight reading" vocabulary.

Each trainee will differ in his ability to learn in the above areas. A wise teacher will give each one the training he can absorb and not waste time pushing him toward impossible goals. The result of pushing is frustration.

A retarded person's desire to learn may motivate delayed development of academic ability. When a twenty-six-year-old graduate of Lincoln School visited his alma mater, he remarked, "Mr. Ginglend, could you teach me to write my name?"

"Of course, George, but you can already write your name."

"No, I print it," explained George.

The teacher gave George a sample with letters of his name written separately and some tracing paper. He told George to trace the letters for a week and then to learn to reproduce them independently. When he was ready to learn more, he was to come back to school.

On the second visit, the teacher gave George a written sample of his name to trace and then to reproduce independently.

On the third visit, the teacher gave George a workbook of cursive writing. George can now write anything he can print.

Who can evaluate, let alone define, the personal satisfaction and sense of worth that this young adult man derives from his ability to write his name as other people do?

Reading, Printing, and Number Skills

Experience at Lincoln School upheld the theory that no one has the right to claim that retarded individuals reach their academic potential by the time they become teen-agers. Several trainees experienced spurts in learning as they were nearing twenty.

One young man did not learn to tie his shoes until he was nineteen, although persistent efforts had been made to teach him earlier. Another man did not learn to write his name until his last year in school. Many trainees in the class added a number of useful words to their reading vocabulary during the course of the job-training program.

Assessing the individual academic abilities and skills of each person in a class can be a stimulating challenge for a teacher. Each trainee is likely to be at a different academic level, and each trainee is likely to have one area of learning in which he is more competent than in other areas.

Because of these differences in abilities (though for other reasons as well), the teacher no longer sets aside blocks of time for group reading, writing, and arithmetic. Instruction and academic drill take place during a work period. The teacher, or an aid, calls a worker away from a task, helps him individually with academic learning, and then asks him to return to his work. Or the teacher may ask a trainee to do individual paper work when he has finished a workshop task.

In all his planning, a teacher keeps in mind the *practical* use factor of learning. There is continual effort to increase sight-reading ability, particularly of words that are needed for daily living, such as names on cans and boxes in a grocery store. There is frequent working with numbers and repeated practice in writing and printing.

Because of the necessity to repeat and repeat practice, a pupil must be presented with a variety of material. Fortunately, excellent printed material is available, much of it geared to the interests of older retarded students. Obtain quantities of it, and use it with a spirit that challenges each trainee to learn and grow.

Increasing Sight Vocabulary

Materials: set of alphabet cards, vocabulary cards for each trainee, index cards or more durable oaktag ones, workbooks and crayons for the trainees able to use them.

The emphasis in a sight-reading program is on basic words that a trainee will use frequently in his daily life. Some trainees can master only a few words; others will master a huge number; and a few trainees will go on to a simple reading program. When selecting material for these readers, choose workbooks related to teen-age and adult life.

A reading program starts with learning the letters of the alphabet. Most trainees in a class can sing or say the alphabet by rote. Introduce an individual to alphabet cards in the correct order. The teacher holds up a card. The trainee responds. If he doesn't know a letter, the teacher tells him.

Later the teacher mixes the cards and presents the cards as before, but in random order. The trainee may hold every card that he names correctly. The teacher makes a note of the letters with which the trainee has trouble and later assigns written or oral exercises that will give the trainee practice in using and eventually learning the letters he found difficult.

Some trainees in need of alphabet practice may enjoy the follow-the-dot alphabet books. A picture emerges when a person draws a line from letter to letter in the correct order. Some of these books show young adults at work and play.

After the trainee knows his letters well, the teacher starts to help him build up his sight vocabulary by preparing flash cards for him. The teacher prints the following on separate cards: trainee's first name, trainee's last name, names of colors, names of numbers, and safety words such as "Stop," "Exit," and "Danger."

The teacher uses the word cards as he used the alphabet cards, adding new words as the trainee progresses.

The trainee, often without specific training, learns to recognize the names of co-workers on sign-in, sign-out slips, the names of commercial products advertised on TV, the names on cans used in class for work projects, and so on. These words need not be added to the vocabulary cards.

Parents can continue at home the program of building up a sight-reading vocabulary. A teacher, however, must explain to the parents what he is trying to do and how he is doing it and caution parents not to overdo practicing. Parents' praise of achievement and interest in a child's progress can add greatly to the effectiveness of a program.

A few trainees may be able to continue to develop traditional reading skills. Workbooks are available in which pictures and directions relate to adult life. A well-trained, perceptive teacher will know when to use this type of material on an individual basis.

Writing

Materials: mimeographing sheets, tracing paper, pencils, paper clips.

If and when a trainee works, he'll get a paycheck. In order to cash his paycheck or deposit it in his bank account, he'll need to know how to sign his name. Being able to write one's name, for signing a paycheck or for any other reasons, is an ego-lifting experience. Nothing adds more to the feeling of identity than to know that one has a name and can write it down.

The ability to write his name may spur a trainee on to writing other words that are often needed, such as his address, days of the week, month, and so on. Like other learners, a job trainee will first master printing.

Make mimeograph stencils of words that a trainee is expected to copy. Leave many blank spaces so that he can practice copying the words over and over again—first his name, then other words. As he gains skill, wean him from his model. Expect him to sign his name from memory. Give him many opportunities to do so in everyday activities. Give printing homework assignments.

Cursive writing is difficult for most trainees, but they usually ask about it and want to try "real" writing after they have learned to print. Make a pattern for tracing—single letters first, then names, then other words. Write large. Clip a piece of tracing paper over the pattern. Tell the trainee to trace the writing. As skill develops, reduce the size of the writing until it fits between the lines of regulation-size paper. Wean the trainee from the pattern when he is ready.

Addition and Subtraction

Materials: box of cards with number facts, objects to be used as counters, lesson copybooks, paper, pencils.

Select ten cards with very simple addition facts such as 2 + 3, 3 + 4, and so on.

Tell the trainee to copy the numbers as they appear on one card.

When this is done, give him a box of counters, such as wooden beads, buttons, or toothpicks.

Give the trainee the following instructions:

"Look at the first number. What is it?"

"Two."

"Right. Put two counters in front of you."

"Look at the bottom number. What is it?"

"Three."

"Right. Put three counters in front of you."

"How many counters do you have in front of you?"

Trainee counts. "Five."

"Good. That's your answer. Write the answer under the line."

"Put the counters back into the box. Copy the problem on the next card."

When the trainee has learned to do the problems one at a time and to work by himself, ask him to copy up to ten problems on a sheet of paper, leaving room for answers, then to determine the answers and record them as above.

When the trainee has learned to do problems fairly well on scrap paper, give him a lesson book with his name and the word "Arithmetic" on the cover. This is his record book.

When the trainee has mastered adding fairly well, introduce him to "take aways." Proceed as in addition. Problem is $5 - 2$.

1. Trainee copies problem.
2. Places five counters in front of him.
3. Takes away two counters.
4. Finds answer of "3" and writes it under the line.

Ready to Work?

When he has mastered this task, he is ready for an assignment of ten "adds" and ten "take aways" at one session on one sheet of the record book. Work of this type makes an excellent homework assignment. The teacher, however, should see that the trainee also does arithmetic in school in order to check his progress in ability to work alone.

Counting and Recording

Materials: boxes, plastic pill bottles with lids, master cards, paper, pencils, magic markers, material to be used as counters, such as buttons, washers, or screws.

Counting and recording is a basic skill used in certain jobs. The setup for a project to develop this skill includes a series of boxes. In each box is a group of plastic pill bottles with lids. In each bottle are a specified number of objects (such as buttons) to be used as counters. There is a master card for each unit of box, bottles, and counters.

To make a unit, take a box and number it "1." Mark "1" on the master card. Then number the tops of the pill bottles with consecutive numbers, for example 1, 2, 3, 4, 5. Put a certain number of counters, for example seven, in bottle one. Record "7" next to "1" on the master card. Continue to put counters into the remaining bottles, recording each number on the master card.

A master card might look like this

Box 1
1—7
2—3
3—1
4—4
5—6

Make up other boxes with differing numbers of bottles and counters in each box. Number each box, and make a master card for each unit. Beginners will use no more than five bottles in a box and no more than ten counters in a bottle.

A trainee adheres exactly to the following method of work, thus strengthening the concept "Certain things are done in certain ways."

1. A trainee sets a box in front of him and then arranges the closed bottles in consecutive order.
2. He writes the bottle numbers on a piece of paper with a dash after each number.
3. He picks up bottle number one and counts the buttons.
4. He records the number of buttons after the number one.
5. He puts buttons back into the bottle and screws on lid.
6. He returns bottle number one to the box.
7. He picks up bottle number two and continues as above.

When all of the bottles have been returned to the box, the teacher checks the student's paper with his master card. If there is a mistake, the teacher may say, "Count bottle three again." If the student has counted incorrectly, he corrects his paper. If the number is correct but does not agree with the master card, the trainee looks to see if he can find a counter on the table or on the floor. If the counter can't be found, the teacher makes an appropriate remark, gives the trainee an "OK," and adds a new counter to the bottle.

It is very important to insist on accuracy, Practicing work incorrectly establishes poor habits, and inhibits the establishment of correct ones.

Money Training

Money is a fact of life, and all people must know how to use it. Workshop directors frequently remark that many trainees have no real concept of money. They don't know which coins to use for the correct bus fare, which coins to put into a soft drink machine, or how much change to expect from a simple purchase. Many trainees are deficient in money skills because they did not learn money facts at school or at home.

There are four aspects to learning the use of money: (1) counting, (2) identification of coins and bills, (3) knowledge of equivalency of coins, (4), arithmetic needed for adding up costs and making change (which is, in essence, subtracting).

Counting Money, Identifying
Coins, Learning Equivalency

Materials: real coins and bills of small denominations.

Most trainees can learn to count by rote to twelve or fifteen and use these amounts accurately. Some will learn to count to one hundred and to count by fives and tens. The dividing line between what is counting by rote and what is meaningful counting is nebulous. The important task is to keep the trainees counting by using a variety of methods that require them to do so.

Most trainees can identify money. To test this ability, the teacher puts a number of coins on a table and says, "Which is a penny?" The trainee points to a penny. The teacher says next, "Give me a nickel." The trainee hands the teacher a nickel. The teacher then tests for identification of a dime and a quarter. He may want to include a half-dollar as a surprise. Not many are in circulation today.

The next task is to teach the equivalent value of coins. This is done by practice. The teacher says, "A nickel is the same as five pennies. Give me five pennies and I'll give you a nickel." Later he may say, "I have a nickel. How many pennies is it worth? Hand them to me." This type of practice continues in as many ways as possible.

Making Change

Materials: real coins, small objects with prices on them, number-fact cards with cent signs.

Making change is a difficult task that some trainees can master. All should have experiences where a teacher and trainee work with real objects and real coins.

The teacher or aide and the trainee take turns being clerk and customer. The customer picks up a can of soup, for example, notes the price out loud, and gives the clerk a quarter. The clerk then gives the customer the exact change, counting out loud. This type of exercise can be extended as far as the trainee is able to go.

Making change can also be taught by using subtraction cards similar to those used in arithmetic lessons with a cent sign after each number. Take each trainee as far as he can go in this area of learning.

Money Concepts

Most trainees grasp the idea of saving money for clothes, presents, and other desired objects that cost several dollars. They should also gain a concept of the cost of groceries and other household expenses. Some retarded people eventually live independently and handle money matters with the help of a social worker or a relative. If retarded persons learn while still in school and living at home that everyday living costs a lot of money, they will be better able to accept the advice of a qualified outsider when they see their hard-earned money being spent for basic essentials, not the luxuries that they'd like to have.

All retarded persons should be encouraged to save some money in a safe place, like a bank account.

They must be cautioned also to carry only the amount of money they are going to need on a certain day. If they realize that all people should take this precaution, they can accept the idea without building up undue fears. Most retarded people capable of taking part in community life know that there are "good guys" and "bad guys" and that some bad guys steal money from people who carry it around.

Pegboard Patterns

Working with pegboards is not child's play. It may be the most important training experience that a worker encounters in mastering the ability to look at a pattern and transfer what he sees to what he is doing. Many workshop jobs demand this ability to transfer from seeing to doing because a number of consignments involve assembling favors or other novelties in a specified way.

In working with a pegboard, the trainee learns to do the following:

1. Follow written directions without being told what to do
2. Work independently and without supervision
3. Do a job to completion
4. Turn in a completed job for inspection. If there is a mistake, the teacher catches it at the end of the job, not while work is in progress.

Other intellectual skills that are constantly reinforced are counting by rote, recognition of colors, sight reading of names of colors, matching colors of pegs and beads that are put on top of them. Manipulative skills that use the small muscles of the hand and eye-hand coordination are also constantly reinforced.

From a teaching point of view, the pegboard offers a unique opportunity to have members of a class work on the same project at different levels. This is important because as members of a class of retarded persons mature, their individual differences in dexterity, stamina, attention span, and other abilities multiply and become more apparent. For the dedicated teacher, this situation is stimulating and challenging, and it can be challenging for the trainees, too, if the assignments are highly individualized and diversified.

The teacher should make up dozens of pegboard patterns geared to the abilities of the classroom members. Lincoln School had a box containing hundreds of patterns. These patterns were numbered on the back for record keeping.

Pegboard Assignments

Materials: a few pegboards with large holes and matching pegs, a pegboard with small holes and matching pegs for each member of the class, beads to match the pegs, three training boards (described below), patterns, work orders.

A teacher must test prior ability of a trainee before assigning him work on a pegboard. Start with a board that accommodates large pegs. Later have trainee transfer to a board with smaller holes and pegs. Give a trainee tasks of increasing difficulty.

The sequential order of pegboard assignments is as follows:

1. Demonstrate ability on a training board, which is a large pegboard with a crayoned design drawn through the pegholes. If a trainee can execute correctly three different designs, he is ready to follow a simple pattern done on a square of paper.

2. Look at a pattern on paper and reproduce it by putting pegs in a pegboard. In doing this, the trainee is matching colors, but he is not using numbers or written words.

3. The trainee is given a written work assignment with numbers and colored dots, but no written words. For example:

> 3 (three red dots, no words)
> 2 (two yellow dots, no words)
> 3 (three red dots, no words)
> 2 (two yellow dots, no words)

He knows that this means to fill the first row with 3 red pegs, 2 yellow pegs, 3 red pegs, 2 yellow pegs. He is matching colors and is learning to associate a numerical value with what he is doing.

4. The trainee is given an assignment that may read:

> 3 red, 2 yellow, 3 red, 2 yellow

(with the name of the color underlined in the color it represents)

This is for the trainee who recognizes numerals and knows colors, but needs to learn printed color names.

5. The trainee has now reached a point where he knows colors, color names, and numbers and can follow a written order with no other visual clues. His assignment might read:

5 red, 2 yellow, 3 blue
2 green, 3 orange, 0 blue, 2 red
and so on to complete the board

Any combination of numbers can be used, but no line must total more than ten, including the zeros. The total can be less than ten, of course.

6. In this assignment, the trainee learns the meaning of the ditto mark. An assignment might read:

5 red 3 yellow 1 blue 0 green
2 " 4 " 1 " 4 "
0 " 2 " 5 " 3 " and so on.

In all of the above steps an additional exercise in color matching can be added by asking a trainee to put a matching bead on each peg.

When a trainee has advanced sufficiently to complete a work order similar to example five, he is ready to use a lesson record book. After he has completed a board, he gives his work order to the teacher. He then opens his record book and writes on a page the date, copying it from a paper if necessary. Then using the completed board as a pattern, he writes down in column form (like addition) how many of each color are in a row. He then counts the total number of pegs in each row and records the number at the bottom of the column. The purpose of this exercise is not to teach addition. The trainee is following a procedure—step by step.

Later the board is checked. The teacher or an aide holds the lesson book and the work order. The trainee looks at the board and calls off the number of pegs: "Two red, three blue," and so on, remembering to say "nothing" or "zero" where there is a blank.

If the teacher feels that a certain trainee needs more practice in color recognition, he can ask, "What color is this?" Or he can use the board in other ways to reinforce learning skills.

Part II
Keeping Fit to Work

Keeping fit to work means keeping physically fit and much, much more. It means developing and maintaining total fitness as far as possible. A lopsided training program can produce lopsided personalities unable to cope with the stress of mingling with other people at work or at play.

There are, for example, throughout the country, excellent programs of physical education for retarded persons. It is possible to develop a particular retarded person into an outstanding physical specimen. But if the instructor ignores totally other areas of development or gives them only minimal and incidental attention, the results could be a superb physical speciman unable to interact harmoniously with fellow workers and unable to function adequately in any kind of social situation—a person whose inner feelings of satisfaction and achievement are so minimal that he experiences little joy of living, a person unable to give expression to or gain relief from emotional pressures.

In like manner, an instructor might train a retarded person to perform a certain job perfectly and produce a rigid self-centered personality unable to work with other people and enjoy his life away from work.

As far as humanly possible, a fitness program must include planning, developing, and evaluating activities that enhance and strengthen physical, emotional, and social growth.

The more a teacher works with retarded persons, the better he realizes the importance of certain established concepts.

1. All aspects of development in life are interrelated. Folk dancing is indeed good for the soul. It is also good for the body, mind, and social development.

2. Development always advances in sequential order, although it may progress at varying rates. A child learns to sit up before he learns to stand. A person is a self-centered infant before he can become an outgoing adult.

3. Development does not occur automatically. It is the result of a variety of experiences that promote growth. A "normal" young person seems to have an inner drive that prompts him to seek out and take part in activities needed by his body, mind, and soul. A retarded person cannot seek for himself, and very often his inner drive has been suppressed or misdirected. He must be given opportunities that help him develop acceptable social attitudes and skills, teach him enough about music, art, and nature activities to make them enjoyable, and sustain enough interest in games and sports to help him keep in good physical shape.

4. Once a skill or attitude has been developed, it must be reinforced with practice if performance is to be maintained or developed further.

In any good program for retarded trainees, job skills and academic training should be mixed with recreational activities that also help prepare a worker to get and hold a job.

Take, for example, Jim, a young man with Down's syndrome, whose main problem seems to be that he is offered too many jobs and he wants to take them all. At present he is working at two drugstores, where he does light cleaning that includes careful dusting of shelves and merchandise. At home he works for a gift shop making ribbon bows on a machine.

"It's bowling that enabled Jim to hold onto jobs," his mother explained.

"Good exercise!" is the natural reaction, because bowling is a physical sport that requires body coordination of torso, legs and arms, and eye-hand coordination. Mongoloids can become lethargic. Bowling certainly prompts Jim to stand and move in a coordinated manner. Many retarded workers give up their jobs for the simple reason that they cannot stand for a period of time.

"Of course, it's good physical exercise," his mother agreed, "but the great value lies in another direction. Bowling taught Jim to accept criticism. When he goofs, his teammates boo."

The ability to accept criticism has to be learned. Many retarded adults can't take it, and they quit jobs even though they can do the work. The attitude can be taught in a trainees' class and reinforced through games and sports.

It's easy to understand the situation. In a loving family, the retarded child is treated as the special child, often receiving special favors and sometimes ruling the roost. For years he attends a special class or receives special attention in a regular class. If these classes remain on a childhood level psychologically, the retarded adult is pushed into an adult job situation in which he is expected to work like anyone else. If the boss bawls out one worker for being sloppy, he'll also bawl out another—even if the worker is a retarded person. Bawling outs are closely related to "boos," and a trainee must learn to accept both with grace and a determination to do better next time. Real-life situations where praise and jeers come naturally do indeed help to teach a retarded adult an attitude that will help him hold onto a job.

While bowling, Jim received other social training valuable on the job. He had opportunities to talk to people—strangers and friends—and learned not to interrupt a person who was busy. He practiced suitable conduct in a public place.

By noting his score and comparing it with his own previous record, Jim continued to use some of his academic skills.

Being on a bowling team was a constant reminder to "do things right." A bowler cannot step over the starting line. He must take turns and keep out of the way of other people. A bowler falls in line with his teammates the same as a worker combines efforts and cooperates with his co-workers.

The above case history illustrates how a recreation program that includes many types of activities can help a retarded person develop and maintain the many kinds of fitness needed for successful work.

In each type of recreational activity, one area of development is usually dominant. In a physical education and sports program, for example, the emphasis is on development of muscles and body coordination. The side benefits are in the areas of social, emotional, and, to some extent, intellectual fitness. In some cases, the side benefits gained from participation may be as important as the obvious benefits.

5. Keeping Physically Fit

Someone has said that increasing physical ability has the effect of increasing intelligence. Psychologists may disagree if they are discussing this claim in terms of basic IQs, but they are likely to agree that increased physical abilities broaden the range of things that can be taught to a mentally retarded person. Physical fitness increases a person's ability to succeed on a job or in other life situations.

Physical training that results in increased stamina and multisensory training that results in improved muscular coordination help a retarded person use his mental ability to its optimum.

It is unfair to assume that a mentally retarded person reaching the chronological age of twenty or twenty-one is automatically ready to withstand the rigors of a full day's work. It is equally unjust to assume that a half hour a week of directed gym activity or an evening of bowling will keep anyone in top physical shape. Every trainee must receive some kind of physical training every day. This does not mean a daily program of Marine training exercises.

A well-planned program in a school situation includes a variety of games, folk dancing, sports, and some well-chosen gym experiences that provide physical exercise and at the same time help a person develop in all areas of growth.

The trainee needs all the help he can get from every angle because, as a rule, mental retardation is only one of his handicaps. In many cases he performs poorly because—

1. his motor coordination and physical stamina are below normal;
2. his speech is often defective;
3. he may have perceptual difficulties;
4. he has been conditioned to failure and therefore has a poor self-image, which in turn may result in bizarre behavior;

5. he has been overprotected and has little understanding of safety rulings; and

6. being slow to react and sometimes clumsy, he has been left out of many traditional recreational activities enjoyed by other youths his age.

Many of the handicaps listed above can be diminished, or at least ameliorated, through a program that presents games and sports in a fun atmosphere in which each trainee feels he has identity as a player and at the same time senses the importance of the roles of other players.

To be in a game a player must learn to:

> Accept rules
> Take orders and sometimes give them
> Pay attention to what is going on
> Take turns
> Help his teammates
> Do his best

In short, he learns the importance of "I" but loses the concept of "Me! Me! Me!"—the center of everything. Through games he can learn to cooperate and in some cases compete, but always with the attitude, "We'll do our best. We'll win some, lose some." This concept can help a trainee accept a job situation as it is.

With the total development of the trainees in mind, some of the objectives of a school physical-education program should be—

1. to improve muscle tone and general physical stamina;

2. to improve large and fine motor and muscular coordination;

3. to improve basic physical skills;

4. to improve game skills;

5. to increase social and recreational skills and develop abilities and interest in hobbies;

6. to develop a positive self-concept in terms of kinds of things one can do successfully;

7. to develop an awareness and knowledge of basic safety precautions in a variety of activities;
8. to develop abilities in terms of cooperation, taking directions, and accepting responsibilities;
9. to develop abilities involved in communications— listening and understanding as well as speaking;
10. to increase ability in self-help in many areas;
11. to develop the philosophical awareness that life is good and that one has many things to give of oneself as opposed to only receiving.

In general, a school physical training program can be divided into two phases: (1) indoor and outdoor activities that take place on school premises or originate there and (2) activities that take place totally away from school.

Developing Physical Fitness at School

Before planning a physical education program for a class of older retarded students, the physical education teacher, with the aid of the classroom teacher, would do well to rate each person in the following areas in order to judge how well he can be expected to perform and to determine which areas of development need to be stressed in training:

1. Basic physical skills
2. Lead-up game skills
3. Game skills
4. Abilities with equipment
5. Any other skills that the teachers feel will help give an overall picture of the trainee

Teachers can use standarized tests for general physical condition. Examples are the Krause-Weber tests and the Kennedy program used in the YMCA.

Program Plan

The physical education program should range from free, unstructured activity (such as shooting baskets in a gym or on the playground) to the development of game skills (such as dribble-shoot) to more organized games. Whenever possible, the fun approach should be used in the game period. This can be supplemented, however, by formalized exercises and use of special equipment geared to the physical needs of each person.

In general, the indoor program will include:

- Activities that lead to game skills, including skills with various kinds of balls
- Games that develop basic physical skills
- Relay type games
- Folk dancing and other rhythmic activities
- Games that can be used at another time (parties or other social activities)
- Some work on barbell, mat work, punching bag, rowers, ladders, exercycles, chinning, and parallel bars. (This type of work should be supervised by a physical education teacher unless the classroom teacher has had special training in the use of this kind of equipment.)

The outdoor program will include use of recreational equipment on the playground and playing games suitable for the area.

Let a teacher remember that walking is exercise and that it can be combined with learning experiences. A person who *can* walk *should* walk as long as he lives. He can learn to like to walk while still in school.

A class can walk to a variety of places near the school, and members can learn to look as they amble. Even on a short walk, they can spot a bug or ant on the sidewalk or path, notice—even in winter—buds on trees, find shapes in the clouds, and so on. Observing nature, or anything else in the world, can be an enjoyable lifelong hobby.

Equipment

A class would do well to have on hand for use in its outdoor and indoor physical education program the following materials and equipment:

6 plastic whiffle balls
1 volley ball
1 heavier kickball
1 football
2 medium-sized balls
1 set of movable rubber bases
plastic bats
1 catcher's glove
rubber horseshoes (quoits) for
    20 players and stands
wooden pucks and 2 pushers
chalk and masking tape
cardboard cones

Cardboard cones are the spools on which commercial thread is wound for use in factories. Companies discard these; obtain as many as possible, since they are also useful for crafts.

Games

Most retarded teen-agers can play games and take part in sports that interest other young people, although they may need to have special help in learning certain aspects of play and to have some rules modified. A number of games and modified versions of sports were included in the authors' *Recreation for Retarded Teenagers and Young Adults* (see p. 154). This chapter will reintroduce the popular kickball and will describe some of the other games that have been developed for use at Lincoln School in recent years.

Most popular games are relay races and games that use various kinds of balls in different ways. Trainees at Lincoln School chose as their favorites baseball, volleyball, and kickball—with variations.

Most of the games used at school are team games, and they can present certain initial problems.

Identifying team members. Often it is hard for a retarded person to remember which team he is on and who his teammates are. It may be a good idea, at least in the beginning of a program, to give teams names and symbols. For example, there may be a blue team and a white team. Each member of the blue team wears a blue ribbon tied around one arm, and each member of the white team wears a white ribbon tied around one arm. These symbols help when sides are changed, as in a ball game.

Choosing team members. There is the manner of choosing team members. Each time a game is played, the teacher appoints two captains, trainees who have demonstrated their ability to carry out responsibilities involved. No one automatically becomes a captain by any system of rotation.

Captains alternately select team members. The teacher asks, "Whom do you choose?" The captain gives a name. The teacher writes the name on a score sheet (see sample). The chosen player joins the team.

If the game requires one or more pitchers, the teacher chooses players able to perform well. If there is one player with such outstanding ability that his presence on one team creates an unfair advantage, the teacher may ask him to pitch for both teams; or if he wants to play on a certain team, he assigns him to a base position rather than allowing him to move about freely in a field. This may at first appear to be undemocratic, but it results in a game that is more fun for all.

In ordinary situations, the captains assign players to their various positions.

If another class is joining the regular class, not competing as a unit, the teacher in charge apportions the guest players in such a manner as to have reasonably balanced teams.

There should be an even number of innings, but there is no need to establish a set number of innings for a game. A game is carried over into a second day for only two reasons: (1) there is a tie score and no time for a playoff or (2) the game must be terminated due to lack of time or an interruption at a point at which the number of innings is uneven.

Score sheet. Because players themselves may forget who is up, a simple score sheet, like the one illustrated, helps a teacher see at a glance which team is up, who is at bat, how many strikes or balls a player has, how many outs a team has, and, of course, what the score is. The score sheet can be used for baseball, kickball, football, and horseshoes.

SCORE SHEET			
1. Mark		1. Angie	
2. Mary		2. Sue	
3. Paul		3. Frank	
4. Tim		4. Debby	
5. Helen		5. Tom	
6. Martha		6. Kathy	
7. Sam		7. Doug	
8. Jean		8. Bob	
9.		9.	
10.		10.	
11.		11.	
RUNS	**OUTS**	**RUNS**	**OUTS**
1. ///	✝✝	1. /	✝✝
2. O	✝✝	2.	
3.		3.	
4.		4.	

The above score sheet indicates that Wesley is pitcher for both teams. It is now the fourth inning, and Sue is up. When it is time for the fifth inning, Tim will be up.

The score now stands at 3 to 1.

Kickball

Kickball is a basic game, with several variations. The playing diamond is similar to the one used in softball, with thirty-five-foot baselines. The pitcher stands thirty feet or less from home plate and rolls, rather than pitches, a sport ball or soccer ball.

In the beginning, at least, the teacher should serve as pitcher and referee. The player who is up stands behind home plate. Members of the opposing team are spread out around the playing field in the most advantageous positions.

The pitcher rolls the ball to the player who is up. The player attempts to kick the ball and then run to first base. In the beginning it is best to allow a runner to advance only one base at a time. A player may run to the next base only when a ball is kicked. No runner may steal a base on a foul ball.

A foul ball is a ball that is kicked in such a way that it rolls to the right of the line between home plate and first base, or to the left of the line between home plate and third base. A player is out if he kicks three times without striking the ball, or kicks three foul balls. It must be remembered that the purpose of playing the game is to give each player a chance to kick and run. Therefore, a ball should be rolled in such a way that the player can kick it if he tries. A very weak kick that stays within the diamond is considered a fair ball.

Members of an opposing team try to put a runner out by throwing the ball to a baseman, who tags the base. After three outs, a new team is up.

Kick Football

Kick football is played exactly like kickball, but without a pitcher. The player who is up holds the football with his hands, drops it, and kicks it. A person who finds this coordination too difficult places the ball directly in front of him, and kicks it.

Kick football is harder to play than kickball, because a football cannot be rolled to a base. It is harder to catch and throw a football than a round ball.

Bounceball

Bounceball is played exactly like kickball except the pitcher bounces the ball to the person who is up, who hits it with his fist. Bounceball is always played on a hard suface, whether indoors or out.

Horseshoes

Horseshoes (using rubber quoits) can be played according to standard rules, but a slight variation gives an additional chance to score. Place a plastic mat under the rubber circle that holds the stake. Score as follows:

Horseshoe touching mat—1 point

Horseshoe touching circle that holds stake—2 points

Horseshoe over stake (a ringer)—3 points

Twelve points make a game at Lincoln School. A teacher may choose a different limit if he wishes to do so.

Captains choose teams. Every member of a team has a turn to toss before the play passes to the other team.

Knock the Thread Cone

Equipment: two wiffle balls and, for each player, a cardboard cone of the type used for winding thread in a knitting mill.

A center line divides the two teams. If no line is painted on the floor for play purposes, use masking tape to mark the line.

Captains choose team members. Teams stand on opposite sides of the room, facing each other. They observe the center line. Any player who crosses that line is automatically out.

Each team forms a line, and each team member places a cardboard cone upright on the floor, between his legs. Each captain holds a whiffle ball. At a signal, each captain rolls his ball, trying to knock over a cone of the opposite team. A ball is always rolled, never thrown!

Each player guards his cone by placing his hands in front of it, at the same time attempting to catch the ball and roll it back. A player may leave his cone unguarded to grab the ball on his side of the center line, but he must be in position, standing over his cone, before rolling the ball to the other side.

When a cone is knocked over, the player who was guarding it picks it up and goes to the side of the room, where he sits and cheers his team.

When all the players on one team have been eliminated, the game is over; the team with any members still standing has won.

When players become skilled, four or more whiffle balls may be put into play at the same time.

A word of caution: Players usually love this game. Don't overdo it! A full period once a week is enough. Occasionally a teacher may allow one short game after an activity planned for the day has been completed.

Relay Games

Because relay games of many kinds are popular and physically beneficial, it is helpful to develop gradually the necessary procedure.

Start out by using chairs. Have the exact number of chairs for each team on opposite sides of the room. Each team sits on its side of the room. At the signal, each captain sends the first player forward to act in the prescribed method of the particular relay. Each of his teammates moves up one chair. The teammate who has finished his play takes the last chair, sitting at the back end of his team. The action is repeated throughout the race, with the captain checking each time, until player number one is again sitting in chair number one.

Hockey Puck Contests

Equipment: two hockey pucks, chalkboard and chalk, or other type of scoreboard, sticks for pushing pucks.

Teams sit in rows on opposite sides of the room, facing an end wall. A scorekeeper stands at the chalkboard, chalk in hand, ready to record each play.

The teacher chooses a captain for each team. The scorekeeper writes the name of each captain on the board so that marks can be made under each name. (The teacher, of course, will write the names if the scorekeeper cannot do so.)

The teacher announces how the puck will be put into play for each round. If necessary, he will demonstrate. The winning play in each case is the puck nearest the end wall.

Each captain sends his first player to stand at the starting line and hands him a puck. Remaining players advance one seat toward the number one seat. Players who are "up" advance the puck as directed. The teacher decides which puck wins, and calls out the name of that captain. The scorekeeper puts a mark under the name of the winning captain. Every player on each team has a turn before the method of play is changed. Some methods of puck contests follow:

1. Players stoop or crouch and push puck with one hand (never throw it) to see how far it will go with one push.
2. Players kick the puck with one kick.
3. Players turns their backs to the puck and kick it with their heel as far as it will go.
4. Players push the puck, just one push, with a pusher as far as it will go.
5. Relay race. The teacher sits on a chair. Each player in turn guides a puck with a pusher down to and in back of the teacher and then returns to the starting place. He must not hit the puck and is out of the game if he does so.

With some groups of players, it may be wise for the teacher to act as referee and ask an assistant or a trainee to sit on the chair.

Games and races that involve pushing the puck with hands or pushers are excellent for building up shuffleboard skills.

Bowling with Cardboard Cones

Equipment: two whiffle balls, thirty or more cardboard thread cones.

The teacher appoints two captains. Each captain chooses members of his team. Each captain sets up fifteen cones in designated places at one end of the room. In a way the situation resembles a bowling alley, since two games go on simultaneously.

Teams line up so that members can take turns. A player from each team rolls (never throws) a whiffle ball toward his set of cones, knocking over as many as possible. Each captain picks up the cones that have been knocked over and sets them aside so they will not be in the way during the next play.

Each player, including the captain on each team, has a turn. Each captain counts the number of cones his team has knocked over, which becomes his team's score for that set. (The teacher can easily spot an error. If, for example, the captain shouts,

"Nine!" and seven cones are standing, the teacher says, "Count again.")

Captains again set up the cones, and the play is repeated. If one team should knock over all of its cones on the first try, it's a "shut out," and the set is over for both teams. Or if one team should knock over all its cones before every player has had a turn, that is also the end of the set.

After the team has rolled three sets, the game is over. The team with the higher total of thread cones knocked down wins the game. (The number of sets need not be set at three. It was a practical number for trainees at Lincoln School.)

Folk Dancing

More than any other activity, folk dancing provides physical exercise and emotional release, and often prompts a sense of social well-being, too, because it's something that people do together in accordance with a pattern understood by all participants. A teen-ager who learns to enjoy folk dancing in school may join other groups and continue to do square dancing during his adult years.

Folk dancing may be introduced by a physical education teacher, music teacher, or classroom teacher. Whatever the situation, the classroom teacher should analyze and appreciate the value of including folk dancing often in the class program. He should also know how to demonstrate steps and formations and call them with the aid of well-chosen records. It would be fun, of course, to have a fiddler come to school and play for a special event.

Retarded persons learn folk dancing just as they learn everything else, progressing from simple forms to more complicated ones. It might be well at the beginning of the year to review a dance with a simple "slide, slide" step. If a dance calls for partners, pair a less able person with a more competent one. It is always a good idea first to listen to the music and get the beat by clapping, then to proceed with demonstrations.

Retarded persons should first learn simplified versions of traditional folk dances. A number of these are presented in two books published by Abingdon: *Music Activities for Retarded Children* by David R. Ginglend and Winifred E. Stiles and the aforementioned *Recreation for Retarded Teenagers and Young Adults* by Bernice Wells Carlson and David R. Ginglend.

Developing Skills Away from School

A large number of retarded persons can and do take part in sports—sometimes with members of their families, often through programs sponsored by various organizations in a community.

If a retarded person has the opportunity while still in school to engage in sports activity in a building open to the general public, it will be a step toward his feeling at ease in a public situation. He will learn how to act and know what to expect not only with the rules and procedures connected with the game or pool but also with the common courtesies that people with like interests extend to one another.

After leaving school, he is more likely to continue with sports he learned while younger than to try to learn new activities in new places.

There is, therefore, a great advantage in having a class participate in sport programs away from the school building. Swimming and bowling for limited periods during the school year are two away-from-the-school activities that can well be worked into the class program.

Swimming

Most Ys, for a nominal charge, will make their facilities available to a class of retarded teen-agers who want to use the pool during school hours. For years, Lincoln School took three classes to the local Y for two-hour sessions on Mondays, in the early fall and late spring. It was felt that swimming during the colder months constituted an undue risk of catching cold.

At the beginning of the year, the school sent permission slips home to parents stating that the swimming program was part of the education program and that all students were expected to participate. Each Monday students wore their swimsuits to school under their clothing and carried two towels and underclothing in a marked zipper or plastic bag. By having students ready to discard clothes, no time was wasted getting ready to enter the pool.

In setting up a pool-use program, it is necessary that at least one leader hold a badge in Red Cross Senior Lifesaving. In the Lincoln School situation, the physical education teacher accompanied the class.

The original intentions of the program were not primarily to teach students how to swim. However, in less than two years, 80 percent of those taking part in the program became swimmers.

Some of the initial goals for the program were—
1. to help students overcome fear of water;
2. to make students aware of the basic safety precautions related to water;
3. to have students utilize various body motions and develop body coordination involved in swimming or trying to swim;
4. to have students experience water therapy, which often improves neuromuscular efficiency;
5. to begin swimming instruction;
6. to present a real-life situation in which students would develop skills in undressing, showering, shampooing, using deodorant, and dressing—all within a limited time.

The program needed a minimum of three adult supervisors. Two were needed in the pool; another was needed outside the pool either to supervise the few class members who were not going swimming for hygienic or health reasons or to be with a student who was hesitant to enter the pool. Sometimes it is beneficial to allow a fearful student to sit with an adult by the side of the pool for a few sessions before encouraging him to enter the water.

The self-dressing program, considered to be vital, presented certain problems—all of them solved with common sense and sometimes with the help of volunteers who realized the importance of the training program.

Male teachers were often few, and male students in the class were many. For a number of years, a parent volunteered to help with the younger boys in the locker room. The school also used other volunteers. In some cases an older student from the regular school was given time off to help, the experience being considered beneficial to both the chosen boy and some members of the class.

In the early stages of the self-dressing program, many of the students needed a lot of direction and assistance. When, however, they learned what they were expected to do and how to do it, many became surprisingly self-sufficient.

One problem—to be expected—was the habitual slowpokes. They were asked to leave the pool five minutes earlier than other class members. They soon speeded up their abilities in showering and dressing in order to be able to remain in the pool as long as their classmates.

Bowling

Most bowling alleys are willing to give reduced prices to groups of students who wish to play during weekday mornings. The price includes scoring pads and use of shoes. In cases where the cost of the activity cannot be included in the school budget, civic groups often underwrite a ten- or twelve-week program if members understand the full value of the program. One year a group of professional women sponsored bowling for two classes at Lincoln School at a cost of $120.

Teen-agers usually enjoy bowling; it can become a life interest pursued with families and other adults, some of whom may belong to special groups.

Besides the fun, which must not be underestimated, there are many other advantages to be gained from a class bowling experience.

1. There is great likelihood of improvement, which, for anyone, means success. The bowler, his classmates, and the teacher can note increased skills week by week.
2. The sport requires use of large muscles and develops coordination of body movements.
3. Each player develops certain responsibilities. He learns the routine of obtaining his shoes and returning them. He chooses his own bowling ball and returns it.
4. He must remember his turn.
5. He interacts socially with his group and with other people who may be at the alley at the time.
6. He remembers his score and, in some cases, records it. His score becomes important to him. Each week he can compare it with his previous score. He may wish to compare it with scores of classmates and also with scores mentioned in newspapers or on TV.

Bowling scores were important to students at Lincoln School. At the end of the bowling program, the teacher totaled individual scores with the idea of giving public recognition to winners at a spring music festival to which parents and sponsors were invited. A trophy and certificate of completion were given for the following: highest individual score; first, second, and third highest scores for men; and first, second, and third highest scores for women. Each remaining player was given a certificate of completion and a token trophy. Trophies were donated by a group that sponsored a Saturday program for retarded youths.

6. Keeping Emotionally Fit

Keeping fit emotionally has many facets. Only one is considered here: continued and expanded enjoyment of music, art, and social experiences that promote sharing activities with other people, development of hobbies, and maintenance of physical skills—especially those related to motor coordination and eye-hand dexterity. Some adult cultural experiences may resemble childhood activities with a switch in emphasis.

The difference between a childhood approach to activities and an adult approach to hobbies is usually more one of motivation than proficiency. For example: a Brownie Scout makes a pinecone troll because she is directed to make a pinecone troll along with other members of her troop, and she receives personal satisfaction in her achievement. A Senior Girl Scout is more likely to make a pinecone troll because she wants to use it as decoration, sell it at a church fair, or give it to a special friend who might get a good laugh out of a pinecone troll. She not only receives satisfaction in her achievement but also in the fact that her pinecone troll will be used in a special way. Retarded teen-agers are like their so-called normal peers in that they receive an emotional lift when doing some fun thing for a purpose.

Because of the psychological difference between teen-agers and children, the motivation for music, art, and social programs for a class of retarded youth must have a different approach than classroom experiences for young children.

The big advantage of including in a class plan group projects related to art, music, and parties is that socialization takes place whenever people work, play, and eat together. The attitude toward doing things together or working toward a common goal can be positive, negative, or just neutral. Individuals need guidance to grow into effective well-adjusted persons.

It is in this area of developing positive attitudes toward life that parents, aunts, uncles, brothers, sisters, neighbors, and lots of other people can help retarded persons most. If these people whom a retarded youth admires, or with whom he has frequent contact, look forward to coming to a program or admire a library window decorated by class members or think it's a great idea for a class to have an alumni dinner dance, class members may become enthusiastic about the projects.

If, on the other hand, parents, school board members, curriculum supervisors, or other people connected directly or indirectly with planning a total program for a class of mentally retarded youth refer to socializing activities as "frills," "busy work," "do-gooding," or just plain "blah," their attitudes will be reflected in the outlook that retarded youth have on life.

Just what specific programs a class can plan to do for other people, what art work they can do for another group, or what social activities they can plan for themselves as a group will depend, of course, upon the makeup of the group itself and the needs of the community in which members live. A wise teacher knows his community and keeps his eyes and ears open to learn of opportunities for his class to be of service.

In like manner, a wise teacher who is fortunate to have the help of special teachers in art and music takes every possible opportunity to plan with them, to follow their guidance to the extent that they want assistance, to understand their professional problems, and to display an interest in what they are doing and why.

The preplanning has two general aspects. The first is understanding the goals of the special teacher and helping him to appreciate the philosophy of the need to develop each student as a total person. It is worthwhile to spend time discussing how the special subject leads to this type of growth.

The second concern is planning specific projects. Very often the classroom teacher can build up general enthusiasm about a project to be directed by a special teacher. At other times, he may provide background information that helps trainees understand a project. For example, most trainees know a lot about the holidays for which people make special decorations and sing or listen to special music. But some class members may know nothing about dragons, which may well be the subject of a song or an art project. A classroom teacher can help sustain enthusiasm about the holidays and build interest in the subject of dragons.

One thing is certain: the enthusiasm of the classroom teacher inspires the special teacher and is reflected in the emotional fitness of the class members.

Although teachers in communities unlike Plainfield, New Jersey, will wish to inaugurate and carry out programs best suited to the needs of their classes, they may profit from descriptions of a few of the successful programs in which trainees at Lincoln School took part.

Music in a Class for Trainable Teen-agers

Everyone needs music as long as he lives. He needs to hum or sing to himself—in tune or out—and he needs to enjoy music in one form or another with a group. Music expresses the soul and rhythm of life.

Every classroom program should include music, but not the same kind of music year after year, and not presented for the same reasons. Music is included in the early years of education of retarded children as a means of reaching out to them, of prompting them to express their emotions and join with a group in making sounds and motions in rhythm and according to directions. Carefully selected songs and dances encourage children to socialize, reinforce many language concepts, and help them improve physical coordination.

Music must remain an important part of the program for retarded teen-agers, but the emphasis is shifted, and material is presented in a different way. In general, there are two types of music in the young-adult program: (1) music for personal fun and relaxation and (2) music that will give joy to other people. The first category includes listening to pop music, folk and square dancing, and singing well-known and much-loved songs. The second category includes programs given for an audience. The class at Lincoln School gives two programs a year: a Christmas program and a program in the spring. Both have different themes every year.

At Lincoln School a "Music for Us" theme was fitted into the weekly programs.

Class members liked to bring their own records to school and listen to them during their period of free time.

At least once a week they had a chance to do what they called square dancing (in reality a variety of folk dances), modified to make them simple enough for the least able members of the class to learn. Little by little, dancers developed a sizable repertoire that they enjoyed with increasing spontaneity. They let off steam in a vigorous and acceptable way; and at the same time, they developed their sense of rhythm, improved their physical coordination, and increased their ability to remember and perform a large variety of steps in different dances.

During the formal music period, the teacher allowed some time for the class to sing seasonal songs and old favorites just for the fun of it. Sometimes when the trainees had finished scheduled work more quickly than usual, the classroom teacher led the group in a sing-along in the classroom.

For a formal program to be presented before an audience, the music teacher and the classroom teacher planned the program together, choosing a theme, selecting the music, then figuring out a way to allow each child to "star" for a moment in some way. For example, two trainees who were particularly good on the drums accompanied the pianist when the class sang "The Little Drummer Boy."

A retarded teen-ager who is blessed with a golden voice should not become a lone star at every class performance. A moment of glory is essential for the emotional well-being of every class member. What about the nonverbal, nonmusical student. Should he be put in the spotlight singing off key? No indeed! There are other ways to give him an opportunity to do something special. One or two teen-agers can hold up a sign or a picture related to the musical number, or produce an appropriate sound effect, play a rhythm instrument at the correct time, or do a pantomime.

After the content of the program has been established, the music teacher records all the accompaniments on a tape recorder. During the music period, the music teacher teaches the class the songs. The classroom teacher, using the tape recorder, repeats instruction at other times. He may also drill the class without the tape recorder, paying special attention to words or difficult sections on which the group needs special help.

The music program gives the classroom teacher a chance to coordinate learning activities around the musical program theme. He works with the art teacher to produce decorations. He can usually find seatwork or academic work related to the musical theme and ask class members to do it.

Presentation of the program need not end with one performance given before the entire school or one performance for parents and friends. Look around the community and see if the music program can offer an opportunity for class members to go as a group to some new place, to meet new people, and to give the audience a chance to enjoy music and at the same time observe how well-trained retarded young people act and what they can do. The Senior Citizens Club was delighted to have the class at Lincoln School repeat its program at the club's luncheon quarters.

A word of caution: Use common sense. Don't let performing dominate the school program or squeeze out other essential types of training. Go only to groups that have given evidence that they are sincerely interested in the school and its training program. If there are a number of requests for appearances, choose the ones that will help retarded people the most in the long run as well as the short run. At different times, the class at Lincoln School gave concerts and other demonstrations for teacher-training classes.

Musical Programs at Lincoln School

The trainable class of older students gave two musical programs a year at Lincoln School, a Christmas program and a spring program. The spring program had a different theme each year. Some they used were "Inside the U.S.A.," "Sing! It's Spring!" "Our Country—North, South, East, and West," "Let's Pretend," and "Music Around the World." More traditional themes might center around Purim, or other festivals celebrated by ethnic groups in the community.

Each program was planned to be more than a musical experience. It offered an opportunity to coordinate and reinforce other types of skills. A description of one program, "It's Christmas," may illustrate how everyone connected with the older trainable class took part in preparing as well as presenting the program, and how nonmusical learning skills were reinforced.

Early in the fall, the classroom teacher and the music teacher chose ten themes (one for each class member) frequently pictured on Christmas cards or in ads. Expressed in rhyme they were:

1. Candles and lights
   Shine in the night.
2. Music and singing,
   Christmas bells ringing.
3. A wreath on the door,
   Gifts on the floor.
4. Santa, old dear, and
   Rudolph the reindeer.
5. Turkey and sweets,
   Lots of good things to eat.
6. Pretty poinsettia, holly so gay,
   Christmas trees trimmed for the big day.
7. Snowflakes dancing and falling around,
   Frosty the snowman is back in our town.

8. Angels singing, high above earth,
   Tell the news of Jesus' birth.
9. Wise men follow a star
   To a lowly stable afar.
10. Baby Jesus, Mary, and old Joseph, too,
    Mean Christmas to me and Christmas to you.

Clues to the program were used Christmas cards. The teacher collected scores. There had to be at least ten for each theme. Because food is pictured less often than other subjects on Christmas cards, it was necessary to cut construction paper the size of cards and paste on them pictures of Christmas goodies such as turkey, cookies, pies, and candy canes. Selected trainees helped do this.

When it was time to talk about the Christmas program, the teacher wrote each verse on a separate piece of paper. Trainees drew the papers by lot. The teacher recorded the name of the student and his selected verse.

The teacher spread out on tables the piles of Christmas cards. He either asked each trainee to read his verse in turn or (in most cases) read it for him. Then he said, "What things are in your verse?" If the trainee answered, "Candles and lights," the teacher said, "You are going to pick out cards with pictures of candles and lights. Choose only candles or lights. Look until you have at least ten cards with a picture of a candle or a light on it. Then take the cards to your seat." The instructions were repeated with each trainee.

When every trainee had at least ten cards with pictures of his theme, the teacher asked each person to choose the card he liked best and to put his name or initials on the back. Then each trainee selected one picture card for each theme. He did not put his name on these. By the end of the session, class members had selected one hundred cards, ten for each theme. Remaining cards were put away.

The next job was to make ten posters that could be placed on an easel. There was a poster for each theme, and each poster had ten related cards pasted on it. In the center of each poster was the favorite card of the person who had drawn the theme. For example, Tom's poster had a picture of Santa Claus in the center. Then, pasted around it in random fashion were the nine other cards that class members had selected. When the program was presented, this was Tom's theme and Tom's poster.

On ten other posters, the themes were printed in large letters. The classroom teacher drilled the students in reciting the ten verses as choral readings. Later, as the ten posters were presented, they would recite the verses in accompaniment.

For practice and for the performance, the posters were placed on an easel in order of their presentation in the program; that is, going from front to back, first a theme poster, and then its related picture poster. The teacher and the class recited the theme and each trainee in turn removed his verse, displaying underneath the poster with related pictures. The class sang related songs. The trainee removed his poster, revealing the next theme.

In this program, everyone had a moment to star as he stepped forward in a dignified manner at the correct time, removed the theme poster, sang with the group, removed the picture poster, and returned to his place with the group. He had to remember at all times that the success of the program depended on how he acted. He could help to make the program beautiful, or he could ruin it by goofing off with silly behavior. Somehow the retarded teen-agers and young adults in this class always managed to express the special joy of Christmas in their musical program.

Arts in an Older Trainable Class

At Lincoln School classroom arts-and-crafts projects were introduced in the earlier stages of children's development to give them experience with a variety of materials and to give them opportunities for imaginative expression. When these children became older, they were still given a variety of materials with which to work, and were encouraged to be creative to the extent of their ability. In planning an arts-and-crafts program, however, teachers became much more selective and purposeful in their choice of projects. For example, class members created large figures and other decorations, made pinecone candlesticks, or did paintings to use as room decorations, gifts, or entries for an art contest.

Art, for art's sake, became incidental; but taking part in art projects continued to play a vital role in helping each trainee develop emotionally, socially, physically, and, to a limited extent, intellectually.

Being able to plan with the art teacher always helped enormously. Both the classroom teacher and the art teacher knew in advance what the major projects for the year would be and therefore assembled needed materials in advance and allotted sufficient time in the lesson plan. Because teachers were never caught short, they avoided the pressure of deadlines for finished projects. The entire class was able to work in a relaxed atmosphere and look forward to a coming event with the realization that the art-and-craft work under construction would no doubt please someone.

General planning for a year usually included:

- Decoration for holidays, with each one listed and specific projects outlined as soon as possible
- Decoration for special dinner party or other social event
- Decoration for annual music program
- Participation in Teen-age Arts Festival
- Special short-term projects.

Art Projects

The trainable class for older students and the children's department of the main library in Plainfield, New Jersey, established a relationship in the field of arts and crafts that proved to be beneficial to all concerned and thus has endured over the years. A few examples will illustrate how the use of class art projects was extended and how appreciation of the work multiplied.

Bong the Dragon

A spring music program given at Lincoln School featured a sketch called "Bong the Dragon," with choral speaking and rhythm band instruments used for sound effects. In preparation for the program, the class of older, severely retarded youth made a huge dragon of double sheets of kraft paper, stuffed the figure lightly with crumpled newspaper, and decorated it with green tissue-paper scales and glittering dorsal appendages. (Kraft paper is a special heavy paper that comes in rolls of several colors. It's useful when creating large-scale figures because it is strong and inexpensive compared to other types of paper used in craft projects.)

The art teacher mentioned Bong to the head of the children's department at the city library.

"What will happen to Bong after the program?" asked the librarian. "Could the library display him?"

"Of course!" Bong hung in the children's section of the main library all summer. Several of the trainees who helped in his creation stopped often to see him because, as they said, "Bong's a friend."

Evidently he was a friend, remembered by a number of families. When winter came and the snow was just right for packing, several snow dragons appeared on lawns along with traditional snowmen.

Christmas Wreath and Stockings

For the Christmas music program, the class made a huge wreath of double sheets of kraft paper, which they stapled together and stuffed lightly with crumpled newspaper. They decorated the side that faced the audience with twisted squares of green tissue paper, glued in place thickly.

A huge kraft-paper stocking, stuffed with crumpled newspaper, hung on either side of the wreath. Each stocking was topped with a band of furlike material, made by gluing small bits of white shiny packaging material in place.

"Would the library like to use the large decorations after school had closed for the Christmas vacation?"

"Indeed!"

In the spring, the librarian asked the class if they would like to make decorations for the summer program. One year the class and librarian agreed on a circus theme, and another year they chose fantasy dinosaurs.

Circus Characters

As a group, class members seemed to be well informed about circuses. Most of them had watched circus performances on TV and seen pictures in books and newspapers. Some had attended live circus shows.

Each trainee decided what circus performer he would like to picture, and assumed a typical pose of that character. For example, the bareback rider had arms akimbo, the tightrope walker had arms spread out for balance, and the Indian raised one arm as if dancing.

In turn, each trainee lay down on a long piece of kraft paper and assumed a typical position for his chosen character within the limits of the width of the paper. A teacher outlined the body with magic marker. There was a variety of characters, including clowns. No circus is complete without clowns, and it's easy to relate clowns to a library's storytelling program.

As each trainee in turn stood looking at his own character, the art teacher made additions to the outline where she and the trainee agreed that it was necessary. For example, she drew a short, full skirt on the basic figure of the bareback rider, baggy pants on the clown, and so on.

The art teacher then marked off sections of the costume that were to be painted, and indicated the color by placing daubs of paint in appropriate areas. In some cases, she mixed special colors to be used.

At odd times during the next few weeks, each trainee worked on his particular character, adding special touches of his own—a glittering tiara for the bareback rider, for example, or a sparkling buckle for a cowboy. The trainees did all the painting except for a few finishing touches (such as facial expressions) that the art teacher added where necessary.

When the figures had been completed, they were cut out and hung in the school cafeteria. There they remained for about two weeks before being given to the library for use in the children's section.

Fantasy Dinosaurs

The project on dinosaurs requested by the library started with books. After the trainees had looked at colored pictures in "easy to read" editions published by several companies, the classroom teacher and class members decided on four basic outlines.

The art teacher sketched the forms on kraft paper. Trainees cut out double figures, stapled sides together, and stuffed the shapes lightly with crumpled newspaper. Trainees took turns painting the dinosaurs weird colors and added teeth and scales accented with glitter.

The teachers and the librarian called the figures "Fantasy Dinosaurs." Indeed they were!

Art Shows

Entering art shows helps a group of retarded teen-agers feel that they are part of a larger community and that people outside their own group have interests similar to their own. If the entries are hung in a public building, as they usually are, participants, including the retarded teen-agers, can view their own work on display—a satisfying experience for anyone.

Getting ready to have a class enter an art show admittedly represents a great deal of extra work for teachers; but very often it is the additional effort that makes the difference between a run-of-the-mill program and an outstanding one—

between a required sitting-out-days-in-school existence for retarded students and an exciting experience that gives something to look forward to now and something to be remembered later.

The teachers' work includes acquiring initial information about the show and its regulations, encouraging and guiding students in the actual artwork, and then mounting the entries for display. The manner in which an art project is presented is always an important element of its effectiveness. In order to bring out the beauty of each entry from Lincoln School, teachers mounted it on heavy paper of either harmonizing or contrasting color and covered it with plastic wrap.

New Jersey Teen-age Art Festival

Each year the state of New Jersey holds a teen-age art festival in schools throughout the state. Each entry is marked with the name and age of the artist and the teacher's name. On no entry is there a notation that an artist is retarded or handicapped in any way. There's a certain gratification, from a teacher's point of view, in having students participate in an event on a par with other students in their age group.

In each community, entries are exhibited in a central place, such as the main library. Retarded teen-agers receive an emotional lift when they go to a public building and see their artwork on display.

A panel of judges selects entries considered to have merit. These are sent to the capitol in Trenton for a statewide exhibit. Every student who has entered work in the show receives a certificate from the state with a note of appreciation.

At Lincoln School, every member of the trainable class for older students worked with the same media and materials and on the same subject. Two of the group's efforts were wash-background pictures and folded, dip-dyed cloth. There was nothing stereotyped about the entries. Each one was unique.

Entering the show was an achievement in itself. The fact that judges liked some entries from Lincoln School well enough to send them to Trenton was an additional source of satisfaction to the artists, their families, and their classmates.

Blown Paint on Washed Background

Materials: heavy grade art paper suitable for watercolor painting, poster paint, large sponge, sponge cut into small squares, drinking straws, electric iron. Before the class meets, thin the poster paint to the desired shades for sky, grass, and earth.

Pictures of oriental-looking trees, made by blowing paint through a drinking straw onto a sponge-washed background, take two steps. At the first session, each trainee prepares a background. At a later session, he blows poster paint through a drinking straw in such a way that it takes the form of a tree.

Cover work tables with newspaper. Give each trainee a sheet of paper, and, as always, have him write his name or initials on the wrong side of the paper. If he cannot do this, do it for him. The trainee turns the paper over to the right side.

Ask each trainee to moisten his entire paper by brushing it from left to right with a large sponge wet with clear water. Then show the group a completed picture with sky above and ground below. Give each trainee two of the small squares of sponge.

A trainee dips one sponge into the blue paint and wipes it across the top of his paper from left to right. He continues until the top half of the paper is painted blue. He must go straight across the paper and not make motions up and down and around. When the sky is completed, he repeats the process, sponge-painting the ground the same way.

If each trainee makes two or three paintings, he can later choose which one he wants to exhibit in the art show. Set papers aside to dry. They will appear crumpled. At a later date, press them flat. To do this, cover an ironing board with a bath towel. Set the iron to "cotton." Place paper, painted side down, on the towel. Iron the paper carefully.

Before the second art session, prepare poster paint the shade desired for a tree trunk. It may be black or green or brown, with a little black paint mixed in. Again cover the work spaces with newspaper. Each trainee chooses one of his printed papers and puts it right side up in front of him.

Put a few drops of the prepared paint on the background picture, a little below the place where the sky and earth meet. Give each trainee a drinking straw. Have him stand up. For some reason the painting works better when one is standing. He blows some paint up for a tree trunk. Then he blows paint in various directions to make branches. Let the picture dry.

The bare-branched pictures are lovely. However, a trainee may wish to sponge-paint pink, white, or yellow blossoms on the tips of the branches.

Dip-dyeing

Materials: two or more colors of dye suitable for use on fabrics, old white sheeting, vinegar, electric iron, material for mounting.

Dip-dyeing cotton material produces unique designs that can be mounted as paintings, hung as wall hangings, used as scarves, or made into place mats or other articles.

Prepare dye according to manufacturers' directions. It can be used cold. Put dye of different colors into small dishes.

Cut or tear old white sheeting into squares, rectangles, or circles, depending on the use to which the finished product will be put. Fold the material as many times as practical. Dip a corner into a dish of dye. Then dip the other corners into dishes holding other colors. If there are large white areas, refold the material and dip the unpainted corners into dye.

Open the fabric. See the design. Let it dry. Later, dip the dyed fabric into a solution of vinegar and water to set the color. Ring it out. Let it dry. Iron it.

Display the finished design as it is, or mount it on background paper. It can also be made into a wall hanging.

To make a wall hanging, take two narrow cardboard rolls from wire coat hangers. Cut them the width of the fabric. Staple or sew a wide hem at each end of the cloth. Slip the cardboard rolls through the hems. Run yarn or decorative cord through the top roll, allowing sufficient length for hanging.

A Very Special Art Show

In recent years, the New Jersey Association for Retarded Citizens has sponsored what it calls "A Very Special Art Show," with entries coming from retarded persons throughout the state. Entries are exhibited in a central area, and the show is given as much publicity as possible. Everyone who enters receives a certificate of appreciation for his part in making the show a success. Students at Lincoln School have entered examples of various types of art work done during the year.

Encouraging students to take part in this particular show has an advantage over and above the benefits received from the art and social experiences. In some cases, parents have become aware of the existence of the state association for retarded people and its units and have been prompted to look into its many kinds of services, especially the recreational programs it offers both to members of school classes and to private individuals no longer in school.

7. Keeping Socially Fit

To be socially fit means more than to be familiar with the amenities of society and able to display them when the occasion demands. Being socially fit means to be a secure individual who wants to be—and can be—a pleasant person with whom other people like to associate, a person who feels at ease because he knows that he looks right and acts right, a person who will not be upset if those around him lapse into the use of words reluctantly accepted, but not condoned, by the stable element of society.

Ironically, society expects more in the line of consistent acceptable social behavior from a retarded person than it does from other people. A retarded adult must look like and act like a gentleman or lady if he or she is to succeed on a job.

With a program that consistently encourages members of a class to be polite, well groomed, and well dressed—and to refrain from the use of profane and obscene language or "dirty words"—most retarded persons in training for the job market can gain a secure feeling about the right way to look, the right way to act, and the right way to talk. The hard aspect to get across is the concept that other people who are "good" in many ways, sometimes fail to act like ladies and gentlemen. The retarded person must refrain from imitating displeasing behavior and say, but only to himself, "Too bad he talks like that. I won't copy him."

It's a sad, sad fact that a retarded person correcting his boss or co-workers is usually ridiculed. A retarded person who uses profanity is often fired.

Lucky is the retarded adult who works in an ideal social climate. Many do. A boss who will employ retarded workers is often a sensitive person who knows how to bring out the best in all persons and helps them to bring out the best in each other.

All too often, however, retarded persons who enter the general job market find themselves among profane, obscene people. A guardian of a retarded person may be faced with making one of two choices: (1) compel his ward to quit the job because the pressure of being with unpleasant people is overly depressing and the temptation to imitate behavior is overwhelming or (2) permit the retarded adult to continue work in the antisocial climate because he has demonstrated that his own feelings about himself are so secure that he can continue to be a pleasant and socially acceptable person in spite of adverse conditions.

Blessed is the retarded adult who develops a deep inner feeling: "I know how *I* want to look. I know how *I* want to act. *I* am a gentleman." Or *"I* am a lady."

In addition to learning the extremes of the right way to act and the wrong way to act, a retarded person must learn that the right way to act in one situation may be the wrong way to act in another. The right behavior for a preschool child is the wrong behavior for an adult. Examples are legion. It's "right" to stand and cheer or boo at a baseball game. It's "wrong" to jump up and call out during a non-Pentecostal church service. A small child looks cute skipping and jumping as he goes down the street. An adult looks ridiculous if he skips and jumps as he goes down the street. He may, however, skip and jump in time to music at a square dance. It's acceptable to call loudly to a friend some distance away in a park. It's bad manners to call out in a restaurant.

Choices like the above must be taught one by one, because a retarded person is inclined to persevere in one kind of action rather than figure out what to do from first identifying a situation and then considering alternate ways to behave.

In a school program, the matter of choosing what is right to do at what time often concerns teasing and "fooling around." It is all right to fool around to a certain extent during a free period in the classroom, but not during a workshop period. It is not right to fool around at all in the lunchroom.

Most trainees quickly catch onto the expression, "There's a time and place to fool around [or yell out, or whatever the behavior may be], but this is not the place." Very often a teacher may need only to say, "There's a time and place to—" and the class will finish the expression in unison, "This is not the place!"

Grooming

Watching the advertising on TV, one might get the impression that Americans are obsessed with body odors, sparkling white teeth, and freshly washed hair. Be that as it may, such advertising does have its effect on retarded teen-agers and young adults. They are aware of the various aspects of good grooming and are receptive to instruction and assistance in these matters.

A person who is clean, neatly and suitably dressed, and whose teeth are in fairly good condition is a more comfortable and often more healthy person than a person who cares little or nothing about his appearance. Because they are older than children and because of their need for privacy, teen-agers are frequently left on their own to care for personal hygienic needs. Many of them, unfortunately, simply do not have the techniques for properly brushing their teeth, washing their bodies, and caring for their hair correctly. Some time in the school program devoted to these aspects of living can yield positive results in helping trainees become better qualified for work and social living.

Some aspects of instruction can be worked into the general class program. A carefully selected film or filmstrip can serve as a springboard for discussion. Films must be prescreened, as many have no relevance to the real-life situation that the trainees are in.

If there are two or more classes for retarded teen-agers and young adults in a school, arrangements can be made for special meetings of girls and special meetings of boys. One teacher can take all the girls into a room and discuss with them such subjects as manicure and use of nail polish, correct shampooing of hair, appropriate use of makeup, personal hygiene, and related subjects. Another teacher may discuss related subjects with a group of boys. A few sessions a year can be effective.

Now and then an outside specialist such as a beautician or nurse can talk simply and directly to the trainees, or to a selected few, and generate interest.

A goodly number of matters related to grooming and hygiene must necessarily be handled discretely on a personal basis. For example, one girl at Lincoln School found it most difficult to get up and going in the morning. It seemed to be impossible for her to allow enough time to get dressed and get to school on time. She, therefore, arrived each day with her hair looking like a bird's nest. The teacher asked the girl's mother to send a hairbrush to school, and the girl spent several minutes upon arrival each day brushing her hair. She decided, eventually and on her own, to push herself sufficiently in the morning to do the needed brushing at home. Similar instruction can be worked into a program, little by little, as situations and opportunities arise.

Clothing. There are two aspects to the study of clothing: choice and care. Some adult member of a family usually selects a wardrobe for a retarded teen-ager. But many persons still in school have their say about what to wear day by day—and rightly so. They will be more comfortable in their selection, and there will be less arguing at home, if a retarded person develops a sense of what clothing is appropriate for a typical situation. Most adults have so-called street clothes, worn to school, work, or shopping; sports clothes, such as shorts, worn only on a beach or in a yard; church clothes; and maybe a few party clothes.

Clothes worn to school should be comfortable and similar in type to those worn by workers on a job. They should be clean and reasonably neat. A teacher may wish to have on hand some needles and spools of thread and an assortment of buttons, so that trainees can sew up small rips or sew on missing buttons if need be.

Retarded teen-agers, like their brothers and sisters, enjoy

dressing up now and then in party clothes, unsuitable for work or play. A good school program will include an occasion or two during the year when trainees can properly wear their party clothes.

Shoe care. Most trainees become fairly adequate in the skill of shoeshining if they receive brief instruction in applying polish, brushing vigorously, and shining with a cloth. A favorite method of practice is to have one trainee shine the shoes of a friend, who, in return, shines his. Once a month is enough time to devote to this skill. However, if materials are available, a trainee may choose to shine his shoes during his free period.

Broken shoelaces sometimes spoil good grooming. It's a good idea to have a supply of inexpensive laces on hand so that trainees can replace broken or knotted laces when need be.

Shaving. At one time it became evident that a number of young men attending the trainees' class at Lincoln School needed to learn to shave. The school became the proud possessor of an excellent electric razor, and after a short period of instruction and inspection, the young men became fairly expert in shaving. The class purchased a pint bottle of after-shave lotion.

The shaving part of the training program soon became unnecessary, as delighted parents discovered that their sons could use electric shavers and bought them as Christmas and birthday gifts or just as a matter of course.

Personal Hygiene

Retarded teen-agers can be taught, without embarassment, that body odor is offensive to other people in a work or social situation and that everyone will have body odor if he does not wash his body and his hair thoroughly. Some teen-agers may be interested in learning that even forty years ago many people had no running water in their apartments or homes and yet they did a good job of washing themselves. People living in large cities often shared one bathroom with a number of families. They took sponge baths in their kitchens. Many farm families had no electricity and therefore no running water. They used very little water because it had to be pumped by hand. Yet they washed themselves well. A person who wants to wash himself well can find a way to do it even if he is part of a large family living in a small apartment or house.

Bathing. Some schools have showers, and every student is expected to shower after an athletic program. This period is a good time to help individuals who need special instruction in washing the body and using a deodorant. Another natural situation is a part of the swimming program.

A certain amount of training of students who need special help in body care must be done on an individual basis. Even schools that do not have shower facilities have lavatories with basins. Male and female teachers, school nurses, and even interested parents can cooperate in helping to train a student who has not been taught at home how to take a sponge bath.

Toothbrushing. Retarded persons need a lot of supervised toothbrushing if they are to develop correct habits and procedures. Because a number of persons have not learned these methods at home, a systematic program must be established at school.

The free period that immediately follows lunch is a good time for this activity. In the beginning, the teacher must dispense toothpaste and supervise instruction. Later, when the procedure has been established, the captain of the week or another trainee may take charge, calling each trainee in turn to come get his toothbrush and brush his teeth. At the completion of the job, he washes out his toothbrush and his glass and returns them to a specified place.

Occasionally a trainee is so absorbed in what he is doing during his free time that he gives only cursory attention to his brushing. He must be sent back to brush for a minimum of a few minutes.

A trainee does the best job when using an electric toothbrush because the up-down motion necessary to proper brushing is almost automatic with an electric brush and difficult to master manually. (Caution: a few people have gums too soft to permit use of an electric toothbrush.)

It was a mother who discovered the value of the electric toothbrush for the class at Lincoln School. When her son had a pre-school dental checkup, the dentist asked why the young man had so many more cavities than he had had at the checkup during the school year. The mother rightly concluded that he had not been brushing his teeth after lunch as he had done in school and probably was not brushing correctly. In discussing the matter with the teacher, she learned of his desire to get an electric toothbrush for the class. She bought one.

The teacher who needed additional brushes did more than place an order with the manufacturer. He explained the class' brushing program to the manufacturer, who sent the brushes to the class as a gift. The school nurse, interested in the establishment of the program, was able to provide the class with a goodly supply of toothpaste.

Menstruation. Mothers of young women tend to worry overmuch about how the subject of the menstrual periods will be handled in a class of retarded teen-agers. In reality, the subject rarely presents a problem.

Explanation about this change in life and how to care for the body should be done at home or, if necessary, by the school nurse. A sensitive teacher who makes a habit of recording the behavior of members of the class usually knows when a young woman is having her period because she may be more tense, nervous, less capable of concentration, and more apt to burst into tears if corrected by her teacher or teased by classmates. Or she may have no change in her behavior and take care of herself with the attitude that menstruating is a natural occurrence for a woman, as indeed it is. In all events, the subject should be treated as a private matter.

Sometimes a parent may think it necessary to send a note to a teacher, telling him that her daughter is carrying extra pads in her purse and requesting that she be reminded to take her purse with her when she goes to the washroom.

Some young women have such a difficult time during the menstrual period that parents choose to keep them home. If indeed there is a real medical necessity, parents' wishes must be respected. But the practice of staying home during a menstrual period for psychological reasons should be discouraged.

Toilet accidents. Toilet accidents that occur occasionally in almost any group of retarded young people are always extremely embarrassing to the trainee involved. A teacher can avoid some accidents and handle other situations with sensitivity and concern by taking certain precautions and creating an understanding of facts that some people have to urinate more than other people do and some people have trouble controlling their kidneys.

The following steps help:

1. Insist that everyone go to the bathroom during the rest-room break whether he thinks he feels like urinating just then or not.
2. Insist that everyone go to the bathroom before starting out on a trip or walk.
3. When it is known that a certain person has to urinate frequently, insist that he go to the bathroom both before and after lunch, at snack time, and at period breaks.
4. Watch for individuals who get so engrossed in their work that they pay no attention to the need to urinate until it is too late. Suggest that they go to the bathroom at intervals.
5. Look for students who seem to feel "under par," but not sick enough to be sent home. Suggest that they go to the bathroom at intervals.
6. Give special consideration to a person with a chronic disorder. Epileptics, and some people with other disabilities, have trouble controlling their kidneys. Ask parents to send substitute clothing and a plastic bag that

can be kept in a locker. When a trainee has an accident, he can change his clothes in a washroom and take soiled clothing home.

Sex-related Behavior

The question of sex education and sex-related behavior in the classroom is bound to arise. The authors believe that formalized sex education is not for everyone, especially in a class of young retarded adults who are at different levels of maturity, have varying degrees of sex awareness, are at different levels in ability to understand the function of body organs in technical terms, and are from a variety of cultural backgrounds. The wishes of parents regarding sex education must be taken into consideration.

Discussion of sex-related subjects in a class of this type should be conducted on a private basis when the occasion arises. The tone should be confidential, forthright, and sincere, never putting a student down because of his sex-related remarks, questions, or actions, and never indicating that sex is sinful.

A great many unfortunate sex-related situations can be avoided in a classroom if sex is deemphasised. Certainly there should be no joshing about crushes, no off-color remarks, no sex-related gestures, or sex-related pictures on display. A class should never be left alone without adult supervision. Another teacher or an aid will often keep an eye on a group if the class teacher must leave the room. Even a teacher with eyes in the back of his head will in all probability run into some situations not appropriate for the classroom, such as kissing and roving hands.

Such acts are usually done surreptitiously and with the instinctive knowledge that such behavior is not appropriate for a work-training situation. A teacher must put an end to the actions without belittling the trainee in front of his peers or making him feel really guilty. Usually a stern look or a terse remark such as "Cool it!" or "Cut it out!" is all that is needed.

Now and then a teacher may meet a situation that requires direct and thoughtful attention immediately. Each case must, of course, be handled with due consideration of the personalities involved. Take, for example, the case of John and Mary, who managed to slip behind the piano when the teacher's attention was diverted during a free period. The teacher soon discovered them involved in deep kissing. They sprang apart guiltily as the teacher approached. The teacher sternly told Mary to sit down in a designated chair, asked an aide to take charge of the class, and directed John into the kitchen. The conversation went something like the following:

TEACHER: John, I don't blame you for what you were doing. Mary is a good-looking girl. But you cannot do this type of thing here and stay in school. Do you know what I mean?

JOHN: Yes.

TEACHER: Do you want to stay in school?

JOHN: Yes.

TEACHER: Can I trust you not to do this again in school? Don't say yes unless you mean it.

JOHN: Yes. But it was my fault, not Mary's.

TEACHER: It wasn't anybody's fault! School is not the time to go around kissing people. Are you ready to follow the rules of our class?

JOHN: Yes.

TEACHER: Good! Go do what you are supposed to do now.

A little later the teacher had a similar conversation with Mary. He made the added point that if it happened again, it would be necessary to tell her mother. No one wanted her to get into trouble, and kissing could lead to other things.

The incident did not happen again, but it reminded the teacher to be more vigilant about not allowing the opportunity for it to occur.

Trips

Knowing about social skills and acceptable social behavior is not enough. A person must have many chances to apply this knowledge by mingling with the general public. It is essential for a person getting ready to leave school to have opportunities to meet people outside the classroom and family.

Most retarded teen-agers who have enlightened and sensitive parents have had such opportunities since they were small. They accompanied their parents to church, went shopping, had picnics at a park, visited relatives, belonged to an organization suited to their needs, and in some cases took trips with the family.

Other retarded teen-agers are less fortunate. Those who have been home-and-school-bound during their adolescent years are likely to remain home-bound after graduation unless they get help while they are still students. Regardless of their prior experience, retarded persons can benefit from outings that are carefully planned. Although trips should be—and usually are—fun, they are not fringe activities, not extras serving to add glamour to a program. Class members can have enriching and strengthening experiences when they visit new places; they see new sights, hear new sounds, and, in some cases, smell new smells. Most of the young people will express their reactions in ways that show their feelings, yet conform to acceptable behavior.

The teacher who is training the group also benefits from taking the young people on a trip. He has a chance to observe them in a genuine social situation, to see in what areas they are doing well, and to determine in what areas they still need help.

One important factor must be considered in planning school trips. Although travel can be broadening, it can also be exhausting! Too much stimuli can be disorienting and confusing for anyone, including a retarded teen-ager. Don't give retarded class members social indigestion by rushing them to too many places either at one time or week after week. Don't choose only spectacular experiences. Go to places within their fields of interest.

The purpose of a trip should be simple, direct, and in some way an extension of class members' prior experience. For example, a wise teacher might take her class to a simple restaurant where choices on the menu are few and food is similar to that served at home and at the school cafeteria. The class will benefit from a new experience of eating together in a commercial place, and they will feel at ease because the experience is in reality an extension of eating together at school. No teacher in her right mind would take her class to a café with a smorgasbord! Strange food and too many choices would lead to mass confusion.

Other types of trips can be like smorgasbords if a group tries to see too much on one outing. A person can absorb only a limited amount of stimulus at one exposure. The best idea is to plan a simple trip, let everyone look forward to it, experience it, and recall it. Repetition of some trips has real value.

Too many trips in a single school year can be exhausting as a single trip that is too elaborate. Little is retained when experience is jumbled and students are tired. Also the basic training program can suffer as a result of too frequent interruptions.

Of course, a group that has learned to travel well together can go farther and do more than a group that is experiencing a first trip. Related experiences can be added one by one to a basic experience. For example, a group might attend a play (carefully chosen) being performed in their locality. Their first theater party should not be preceded by dinner. Later on, the group might be able to eat together at a simple restaurant and then go to see a play.

A trip can be simple and direct and still present multitudinous opportunities for promoting social maturity and helping a retarded person adjust comfortably to new situations. Consider some of the ways that a class at Lincoln School benefited when members went by bus to the home of their former teacher, now living at the Jersey shore. This trip was taken near the end of the school year after the group had gone bowling and swimming on a regular basis away from the school building and had successfully taken a few other short trips.

First of all, there was the joy of seeing their old friend and former mentor, a rewarding emotional experience in itself that made the trip worthwhile. In addition, the trip reinforced former experiences and offered new ones. For example:

• The bus trip was slightly longer than any trip they had taken before. It stretched the travelers' endurance a little, but not too much.

• Class members behaved like ladies and gentlemen, as was expected, but in a home they had never before visited.

• Since ocean swimming was on the agenda, students used their learned skills in changing clothes and later showering and getting into their street clothes—but, all this occurred in a new place and under slightly different conditions.

• They jumped, and sometimes swam a little as they had done in a pool, but in salt water with waves, quite different from the fresh, still water of a pool.

• They felt the sand of the beach in their toes, saw the waves and heard their roar, watched sea gulls flying overhead—all new experiences appreciated by those who on their visits to parks had been encouraged to feel wet grass, really look at the world around them, and listen to the sounds of nature.

One experience backfired. After eating a lunch topped with large servings of ice cream, the group went to the combined gift shop and lunchroom at the beach. Each person was given a small amount of money, and it was expected that he would buy a souvenir or postcards as a memento of the trip. The group was told, "Buy what you want with the money you have." Everyone wanted the same thing and bought it. More ice cream! The classroom teacher discovered an area of training that needed to be developed—the wise use of money.

Some other types of outings that trainees at Lincoln School have had, though not all in one year, include visits to—

workshops	private homes for cookouts
theaters	small museums
zoos	farms
parks	story hours at the library

They also attended swimming parties, took rides on trains and ferryboats, and went on picnics. The class also visited a group of young people at a social affair and later entertained them.

Encouraging the Association of Alumni and Students

Encouraging alumni and their former classmates to associate in school as well as in community-sponsored events can produce results beneficial not only to these two groups of young people but to the school's teachers and administrators. This type of contact often helps to form a bridge between the world of school and the world of work.

Being with alumni can give a student a comfortable feeling, a certain kind of security: *everything* won't change when he leaves school. He can come back to school for a visit. Maybe he'll see his friends in other places. The association may give him a glimpse of what the future holds for him. There is bound to be the question, "What you doing?" the answer, and then, "You like it?"

For the alumni, there's the emotional lift of renewing old friendships. And for teachers and administrators there's an opportunity to learn from alumni something about the efficacy of the school program.

Arrangements for alumni and students to come together can be made in a number of ways, including having alumni visit the class on a limited basis and sponsoring an annual social event arranged by class members; for example, an alumni dinner dance or, in some communities, an alumni dinner followed by other suitable entertainment such as a sing-along or some other entertainment that reflects school experiences enjoyed by both present and former class members.

Lincoln School frequently encourages its graduates, especially those who are not working, to visit the class at times specified by the school. As a rule, a graduate takes his place at one of the work tables and does much as he did in the past. The conversation is usually a lively exchange about what he has been doing.

Sometimes when a teacher hears that a recent graduate is having difficulty in adjusting to "no more school," he calls a parent and asks if the alumnus would like to spend a day with his former classmates. Visits are enjoyable times for all and are especially valuable to the graduate, who gains a sense of continuing friendship and identification with his group.

The limitations of this arrangement are obvious. The graduate who is working in either a sheltered workshop or on a private job is not free to visit his former classmates during school hours. An annual dinner party, given in the evening, provides an opportunity for all alumni and students who wish to mingle, to do so. At such an event, a student who asks, "What you doing?" gets an answer "Workshop" or "Working at hospital" or something else. An affirmative answer to the next question, "You like it?" gives the student a feeling that the world of work may have something real to offer him.

An annual dinner party of one kind or another has many benefits besides the joy of renewing friendships and gaining assurance that life after school can be enjoyable or at least tolerable.

1. *From the students' point of view.* The dinner party is similar to events given by and for other groups of teen-agers and young adults. Class members identify with other young people their age.

By making and carrying out plans for the alumni party, students are prompted to plan for other people and thus become less self-centered.

2. *From an educational point of view.* By coordinating a number of assignments around a central theme of the party, teachers have an opportunity to encourage students to reinforce, in a natural way, writing, art, music, social, cooking,

and other skills. Writing lessons can include writing names on invitations and place cards, and artwork is created for a purpose—making decorations for dining-room walls and windows, dining tables, and the dance hall.

Music includes a review of dance steps or familiar songs.

The class decides (and practices in advance) how to set the tables and prepare the food that will not be furnished by outsiders.

3. *From the observer's point of view.* Another dimension is added to the value of the project if there are honored guests such as school administrators, key members of the school board, and other people who have shown an interest in retarded people.

As they sit at a head table observing students in a natural way, school administrators can see in a dramatic fashion the results of the school program that was designed to help retarded young people enter an adult world.

Other guests can see for themselves that retarded people can be helped to enjoy life and to get along with other people.

Publicity for the event can bring about good public relations, promote general understanding, and sometimes prompt additional people in a community to support programs that aid retarded persons.

Although the students at Lincoln School do all of the advance work, they are guests for the evening. Some years parents, and at other times members of a service group, have prepared some of the food, served it, and done the kitchen cleanup. Members of the service group seem happy to have found a project of genuine value, an undertaking in which they were truly helpful in some way other than raising money.

Several procedures have helped to make each alumni dinner party a success. They might well be followed by other groups giving a similar event.

1. The party always has a theme that is carried out in decorations, table settings, and on a mimeographed program. Because of the emotional lag that often occurs during the

months between Christmas and spring, the party is given during the winter, when a Valentine's Day, St. Patrick's Day, or seasonal theme is appropriate.

2. The seating at small tables of class members and alumni is carefully planned, taking into consideration a number of factors that include personal compatibility, similarity of interests, and certain psychological factors. Any teachers who have indicated a desire to attend are placed at tables where trainees might need assistance of one kind or another.

3. On the night of the party—and this is most important—care is taken to help alumni and class members make the transition from the known to the unknown (that is, from a familiar experience to a new experience) and to shield them from needless confusion. Young guests are asked to meet first in their classroom, where they talk to each other and play some favorite records much as they have done during the leisure period of the school day. Other guests meet in the dining room.

When word arrives that everything is ready in the dining room, young guests line up behind the classroom teacher with a dependable class member in the rear. They troop into the dining room and find their names on place cards.

4. There is a variety of dancing—including modern dancing, folk dancing, and musical circle games—in which everyone participates. No one who wants to take part is left out because he doesn't know a certain step or square-dance call.

5. Dinner is served promptly at six o'clock. During the dessert period, the classroom teacher goes from table to table introducing graduates, telling what they are doing and adding a humorous anecdote about their school days. Each graduate rises after his introduction, receives applause, and thus basks for a brief moment in the spotlight, an experience of recognition that everyone needs now and then.

6. Dancing follows dinner and ends at nine o'clock. Before nine-thirty, everyone is on his way home. Entertainment of this type makes for a highly stimulating and active evening. Care must be taken to stop before guests are exhausted.

Part III
The Future Is Now!

No language is strong enough or urgent enough to make the point clearly and absolutely that the transition from the world of school to the world of adult life is all-important to the retarded person. The kind of world in which he will live as an adult depends on what kind of help he gets during the transitional period.

His adult world may be one that is satisfying, purposeful, and useful to him, joyous to his relatives and friends, and pleasant to his acquaintances and casual contacts; or, it may become a life of increasing frustrations and boredom. Even more horrible, it can become a life of increasing behavioral disruption and disintegration.

Most severely retarded persons who have received consistently beneficial training and have had the help they needed at the crucial point of changing from the school to the adult world take the step quite naturally—indeed, it is a natural step—and proceed to live satisfactory lives. A few retarded persons find the transition overwhelmingly difficult despite the most constructive efforts of concerned people to help them mature. Such a situation must be accepted with regret, not bitterness, and with the realization that given a set of circumstances and the light of present knowledge of human development, everyone had worked to the best of his ability.

However, no person, regardless of the degree of his maladjustment, should be discarded as a failure; people must continue to try to help him. And no one specific case should be cited to belittle efforts to train retarded persons for adult life and then ease their entrance into the adult world.

Even with the best of training, the best personal adjustment, and the best health, no retarded person can pretend to fulfill the American fantasy of "pulling oneself up by one's own bootstraps." He needs help! Planned and coordinated help, with no foolish notion that "maybe things will work out for the best."

The retarded person must get help from at least three sources if he is to make successfully the transition from school to adult life. These are:

1. The schools
2. Parents and other relatives
3. Agencies and community groups

8. What Schools Can Do

Our last three chapters will focus on exactly what schools, parents, and agencies can do.

In the complex society in which we live, schools must accept the responsibility for more than superficial training in the three Rs and in vocational exploration. Schools, from preschool groups to colleges and universities, have traditionally been places for persons to grow emotionally, socially, and physically as well as intellectually. Too often, however, the first three areas have been left to chance, and have not been carefully thought through in terms of their weight and role in a school program. In recent years, society has begun to attempt to understand what cultural deprivation and social and emotional maladjustment can mean in terms of a person's total development, particularly his learning and behavioral adjustment.

As a rule, the retarded person cannot consciously aid a teacher in understanding his problems; but he is constantly giving signals—by his behavior and in other ways—that he needs help. Help him we must!

Before discussing any specific methods for developing occupational skills, educators must address themselves to the interrelationship of deficiencies and problems in the areas of physical, emotional, social, and mental growth. Often there is a chain reaction. In its most simple form, a boy is upset emotionally because he can't kick a ball. Because he is upset emotionally, he reacts antisocially and hits a classmate who had nothing to do with his failure. Because the classmate then gets "mad at him," he can't concentrate on a printing assignment.

The reasoning seems apparent, but in far too many school systems the need for a balanced program is overlooked. The superintendent who wants to prepare retarded persons for useful adult life must insist that the curricula provide balanced opportunities to produce maximum development of that loosely used term "total potential." Any program that stresses only one area of development or that overlooks one area of development is bound to fail.

In order to be able to insist on balanced curricula, school principals, supervisors, and other administrators should have a thorough understanding of what is involved in the retarded person's special kind of development and be able to recognize, aid, and support teachers who have the special kind of knowledge and understanding to deal with it. They should encourage a teacher who shows potential in a special class assignment, and they should aid her professional growth.

At the same time, administrators should be able to spot teachers who, because of temperament or motivation, seem unable to develop any special understanding of the needs of retarded persons. They should have these teachers transferred to positions better suited to their personalities. They might, for example, want to replace:

1. The emotional do-gooder who feels sorry for the people "forever children" and does things *for* them rather than insisting they learn to do things for themselves and for other people.

2. The lazy teacher with the attitude, "I'll take them as far as they can go in the three Rs and keep them happy. Why bother with the mess of nuts and bolts? Most of the class will stay at home eventually or end up in institutions. Let the workshops train the others who have any skills."

3. The display teacher who wants to make a name for himself with innovations for the sake of change or publicity. Examples are numerous, for the temptation is great. Typical would be the teacher who starts a money-producing workshop with little thought for overall development of members of the class, the teacher who produces a crack drill team at the expense of other types of training, the teacher who takes the class on trip after trip in order to "make up for the things other kids do that they never get a chance to do."

In short, administrators must find teachers who have goals

that are aimed at total development of every class member, plans that will help implement the goals, and personalities and professional skills that will encourage class members to mature.

In many school districts, the superintendent of schools must defend the budget for a training class not only in human terms but also in terms of dollars and cents. He must be well informed about the scope of the program and how its implementation may lead to employment of retarded people and most certainly to their increased ability to care for their own needs, thus permitting members of their families to work outside the home if they so wish.

Community support comes most easily when community service is woven into the curriculum. The trainees need to know that giving of one's self, individually or as a group, is a part of positive living. The community needs to know that retarded people can be an asset to the community.

Some projects, such as the envelope-stuffing mentioned earlier, are complete in themselves. Others may be of a cooperative nature. For example, a clinic for crippled children might need a certain type of chair too expensive for the budget. A service group might be willing to buy lumber and have parts of the chair precut. A class might assemble the chairs and finish them.

If retarded people are going to take their places as contributing adult members in society, they and the community at large must understand each other. The schools should be the liaison.

The type of training given in a school is important, as we have explained. Community understanding of the special group is essential. But school training and community understanding of the group are not enough. The time comes when a retarded person tries as an individual, not as a member of a class, to find a job. Here is where the school must help the *individual* more than ever before!

In this book, we have attempted to describe how an occupational training curriculum can provide opportunities for development of trainees' total potential in an atmosphere that makes the program a vital satisfying experience and at the same time produces a comprehensive evaluation of each individual's strengths and weaknesses that will enable families, agencies, and communities to better understand him and help him in significant ways.

Schools are in a unique position because of their capacity to act as liaison between graduating trainees and agencies and community programs that may help retarded people during their adult years. Having worked with each individual, sometimes for as long as fifteen years, teachers and administrators are often able to give useful information about a class member. They can spell out exactly where each one's abilities lie and under what kind of supervision he works best.

A school should keep on file application blanks for the services of the Vocational Rehabilitation Agency, and in the beginning of the trainee's final year, should assist parents in making an application—preferably adding a résumé of the school's evaluation of the candidate's abilities.

The school should, if possible, set up a meeting between parents and a representative of each agency that may be able to help a trainee find a job. Many agencies will send to such a meeting a speaker who will explain the services offered and the methods of administering them.

The school should help parents obtain a social security number for a trainee who does not have one.

Teachers should encourage parents to try on their own to find part-time or full-time employment for a graduating trainee, and a teacher should be willing to follow through on any parent's request for an evaluation of an applicant's ability to do a certain type of work.

Teachers in this specialized field should be familiar with recreational services in the community and should recommend them to parents, urging them to have their children continue to mix with people outside the family and remain physically active.

Schools can profit greatly by some kind of follow-up on its graduates. This offers one kind of indicator of the effectiveness of the school program. Also it is human and kind to show continued interest. Let the graduates know that the former teachers and administrators care about their progress, and let present trainees discover through association with alumni what life in the postschool world may be like.

It must be pointed out that the best kind of school training program loses some of its effectiveness if there are no opportunities in a community for sheltered or private employment.

9. What Parents Can Do

To parents falls the most difficult job of all, that of coping with their deepest emotions in an effort to become reasonably objective about their offspring and to try to help him develop a way of adult life that is best for him. This frequently means discarding preconceived ideas and falsely held expectations about what a retarded person should be able to do, facing the situation as it is, and helping their offspring to make the best of it.

It's hard—no doubt about it! No wonder many parents fall into one of two psychological traps.

1. They refuse to truly admit that retardation makes any difference. They say, "If properly trained, he can do anything anyone else can do." Wrong, he can't. Trying to make him fit into a preconceived mold will lead only to frustration.

2. They say, "Poor thing! He can't do much of anything and shouldn't be expected to try." Wrong again—in all likelihood he can do lots of things, and he should, in order to avoid stagnation.

During the years an adolescent retarded person is maturing, his family must try to loosen apron strings without removing love and support to the degree that is needed. They must try to understand what the school is attempting to do, to privately evaluate it, and, if in accord, to supplement, broaden, and reinforce the experiences that strengthen purposefulness and maturity and help make the trainee as independent as he is capable of being.

Parents should also, in a noninterfering way, exhibit support of teachers and school officials who are trying to bring about better individual development and ability.

Perhaps the biggest role that parents can play in preparing an offspring to enter the working world lies in the area of attitudes. Children tend to reflect their parents' outlook on life.

The first important attitude is the way of thinking about work.

If parents truly believe that any useful work—no matter how menial—is important and honorable, their retarded offspring may be willing to do the job that he can do well, happily.

Second, if parents feel that money is important, but not all-important, a retarded worker may be happy to earn what he can.

Third, if parents look for the best in people around them and work in harmony with them, the retarded worker may also be able to work without picking out one fault or another in fellow employees.

If parents express negative attitudes toward work and work situations, the retarded member of a family is likely to do the same. In the case of a retarded worker, a negative attitude toward life may lead to job failure.

Another attitude that parents can help a retarded person develop is regard for authority. This, too, starts long before a trainee is ready to apply for a job. Parents can create a general feeling that the teacher has good ideas. This is another beneficial angle of the aforementioned concept of "reinforcing" the school program. Certainly parents should follow through on every aspect of the school's health, personal hygiene, and social behavior programs. Learning skills can also be reinforced at home. If a trainee learns in school how to mix frozen orange juice and water, he should have a chance to make the drink in the family kitchen. If he learns at school how to set a table in the traditional manner, the family should say, "This is the way we'll set the table at home" and thereafter let the retarded member of the family take his turn in doing it. If a teacher asks parents to help drill a trainee in word reading, they should follow through gladly.

All of the above family activities do far more than teach the retarded member of the family to do useful things. The fact that the programs originated in school underscores the concept, "You must do what the teacher says." This concept can be extended in a natural way to "A worker must do what the boss tells him to do."

When the time comes to help a retarded offspring enter the working world, parents must realize first of all that each retarded person is an individual. The fact that one person with Down's syndrome can and does do a certain job does not mean that another person with the same affliction can do the same job. The fact that a sheltered workshop in such and such a city hires a certain number of retarded persons of a specific type does not mean that another workshop can fit a specific applicant into its program.

A parent must make an effort to understand his child's potential. His best help will come from the school. At this point he must listen, not argue about what he thinks the child's real IQ or his physical ability may be.

A parent must try to learn about all the resources of his community, including opportunities for a retarded person to work part or full time in a private situation or for a small business. A parent must not sit by and lament, "Society ought to . . ." Society needs prodding if it is going to employ retarded persons. The best prodders are parents, and the best persons to prove that retarded people can work are trainees who have not only developed useful work skills and good work habits but have also matured physically and socially to the extent that they have become dependable and likable employees.

Parents who live within walking distance of public transportation must take the responsibility of teaching their retarded child to travel by bus or train. Many employable retarded adults are not able to take advantage of sheltered workshop facilities because they cannot get there by themselves and because family members are unable to chauffeur them at the required time. This training should start long before a person gets ready to apply for a job.

Travel, of course, should mean going someplace a person wants to be, not just traveling to learn to travel. A parent can usually find some beneficial program that meets on a Saturday or Sunday. If it is possible to get there by bus, the parent and the teen-ager should go that way. At first, they will go together, with the parent calling special attention to bus number, important landmarks, and stopping place. She may wish to say to the bus driver on entering the bus, "Please call Thirty-fourth Street" (or whatever the stop may be). However, the teen-ager should know the landmark so that he can get off at the right place even though the bus driver forgets to call. Once off the bus, parent and teen-ager walk to the correct building, again noting landmarks.

On a later trip, the parent will ask the teen-ager to name the bus number, getting-off place, and landmarks, and require him to ask the bus driver to call the stop. Parents have used different ways to make sure that a teen-ager arrives at his destination when he starts to travel alone. Eventually a parent will assume that the teen-ager arrived at his destination safely, just as later on she will assume that as a worker he will arrive safely at his job each day.

Some retarded workers learn to travel by train as well as by bus. They are taught by essentially the same methods.

It is also up to the parents to see that their teen-ager is enrolled in some type of recreation program. The young adult needs companionship, and he needs exercise. All parents should join the National Association for Retarded Citizens as soon as they learn that their child is retarded. However, it's never too late to join. The organization, which has chapters in all fifty states, can, through its many programs, give parents guidance. Most of the units have recreation programs for retarded teen-agers and young adults and also act as referral agencies for other local organizations serving the same people in different ways. If a community does not have a chapter, parents may wish to drive to a nearby locality or start a local chapter. If no chapter is listed in a local telephone book, parents may write to NARC, 2709 Avenue E East, P. O. Box 6109, Arlington, Texas 76011.

If parents are churchgoers, a retarded child of any age will benefit by knowing that he is a part of an extended family—the members of his church. For some reason that need not be analyzed, a retarded person seems to benefit spiritually when he enters the atmosphere of a church and takes part in a service.

Various kinds of Ys and other organizations often open their doors to retarded young people, especially those with special skills and intersts.

Some parents may have to face the fact that there is no employment for their adult children in their community at the present time. This does not mean that the young adults should not work or that their occupational training has been futile. They can and should work at home and in their community as volunteers.

Every member of a family, including the retarded adult, should pull his weight when it comes to chores at home. If he has been able to go to school, he is able to take care of his room, and should be expected to do so whether he is employed outside the home or not. He should take his turn at setting and clearing the table and doing other things he is asked to do. If he has not been able to find employment outside the home, he should help with general housecleaning. This does not make a slavey out of him any more than cleaning makes a slavey out of his mother or his father.

Parents should harbor no sense of imagined disgrace at having a member of a family clean for pay outside the home. The one area of work in which there is acute shortage in the United States is domestic help. Many people want domestic help, and some who are disabled in one way or another need it desperately and are willing to pay someone who works well, even though he may need supervision.

Retarded adults living in the suburbs should do their share of yard work, and retarded people living on farms should have special chores. Some retarded farm workers, living at home, are given their own spheres of work from which they can earn their own money; for example, caring for hens, gathering and keeping a record of eggs for sale, or growing garden vegetables to be sold at a stand.

Other young adults, with the help of parents, may be able to sell handmade articles on consignment. One young woman with special finger dexterity collects shells near the condominium where she lives. She has learned to make beautiful shell jewelry and Christmas ornaments, which are sold easily through boutiques. An alert parent can, and should, find many opportunities for a retarded member of a family to do a variety of work at home.

The retarded adult, employed or not, should also work as a volunteer in his community. There is no better way to make him feel he is a part of society and no better way to help society realize that a retarded individual can be a pleasant and useful person. Almost every type of organization needs volunteer help.

Church, for the most part, offers great opportunities for people to do volunteer work; and church members during the past thirty years have become increasingly enlightened about the role that retarded people can play in the life of a church. As a rule, church members encourage a retarded person in the congregation not only to worship with them but also to join them as they play and work together. There is always work to be done in a church organization! Any teen-ager or young adult, retarded or not, can be a big help.

Many churches give dinners, either purely for fellowship or to raise money. For any dinner, tables must be set, napkins folded, food prepared and served—all jobs with which the retarded adult can help.

Many churches send out newsletters. A retarded adult who has been trained can collate and fold as well as any other person connected with the church. And there are always the eternal cleanup jobs. Cleanup should not be a chore assigned regularly to the retarded person, but it can be a chore shared by the retarded person, his dad, and other men of the church.

Many church members work for months preparing for bazaars or fairs. With encouragement and advice, a retarded adult can contribute her share of articles for sale, for example, dried flowers and weeds, potted plants, and handcrafted articles. The contributions help raise money for the church; and, in making them, the retarded adult keeps alive skills learned earlier in life.

One retarded person who lives with her mother in a retirement community delivers group notices to each house. The opportunities to do community service are innumerable. A list of volunteer jobs that a retarded person could do would be extensive.

Other retarded persons do work on a friendly basis. One man with Down's syndrome goes each morning to a garage and auto-sales establishment where he is given a list of orders for the coffee break and sufficient money to fill them. He goes to a nearby coffee shop where the order is filled and paid for. He returns to the shop, where he stays for a brief time looking at new cars on display. He receives no pay. The men give him clothing for a Christmas present.

It's not an ideal situation. No doubt he is underemployed, but it would be a shame to call it exploitation and force the retarded man to sit at home. He enjoys his contact with other men. He loves to look at new cars and knows a lot about those on display. But he isn't hanging around the showroom. He has a business to conduct there. He has a reason to dress neatly each day, walk to certain places, and walk home. He enjoys the thanks of the workers, and he deserves it.

Some people, especially those who live in rural or semirural areas, may find that training opportunities do not exist in their public school systems. Or they may discover that the goals of a program are quite different from those described in this book. Parents can do much at home to help a retarded teen-ager develop skills described in the first part of this book and to grow into a well-rounded person as indicated in the second section. Certain pointers may help.

1. Begin in a small way. Start with some activity that a trainee can do. Make work periods of short duration.
2. Later, increase the difficulty of the work and the length of time that he is expected to work.

3. Remember that work should be interesting and satisfying to the trainee. Your own attitude of "work is work and fun is fun" can be a guide to encourage him to keep working until an assigned job is done.

4. Be sure to have fun with him. Make him a contributing member of the family and of the community. See to it that he has some kind of physical activity regularly.

5. Try always to help him become as mature and independent as possible. Let him make choices when he gives evidence that he is able to handle a situation in the expected way.

6. See that he is included in some kind of community group. He needs the fellowship, fun, and stimulation of group activity.

7. Try to find some way that he can work outside the home with either a full-time, part-time, or volunteer job.

10. What Agencies Can Do

Like schools and parents, agencies may play a major role in determining what kind of life a retarded person will lead after he leaves school. It's an awesome responsibility, and most professional workers take the assignment seriously, doing the best they can within the limitations of budgets and facilities.

Most agencies and professional organizations concerned with mental retardation serve as clearing houses for services available in a community. They are familiar with the particular setup of workshops in an area and may know of other job opportunities. They know what funds are available for training a retarded person on a job. And they are trained professionally to test an applicant.

There are two ways in which many agencies could increase their effectiveness in doing the maximum that can be done to aid a maturing retarded person:

1. Cooperate more fully with schools, other organizations, and parents who have the same goal. Putting aside vested interests and the temptation to be *the* authority in analyzing an applicant's ability, avail themselves of all the information that can be gathered from teachers and others who know the applicant well, and then make their final decision. (Agencies would also do well to seek the support of the community, schools, and parents in understanding the need of a retarded person to work; and when they get such support, to show appreciation.)

2. Avoid making hasty decisions regarding the ability of an applicant. In placing him in an evaluative or trial employment situation allow time for him to overcome the confusion and strangeness of a new environment and the nervousness he is bound to experience along with it. Think what it means to him to be confronted with new and complex stimuli.

Knowing how to be supportive in a firm and understanding way at this crucial point in a trainee's life may make the difference between his leading a productive adult life and merely existing.

In Conclusion

May we make one last plea to agencies, schools, and parents. Do the best you can to help retarded people make the transition from the world of school to the world of work. Don't be overcome by lack of apparent opportunities or facilities, or by misunderstanding in a community. Your continued efforts are important. Keep trying.

The retarded person, like everyone else, has only one life to live. In the words of the late Pearl Buck, "Their lives can be made to count; they need not be wasted!"

Appendix I
Aids to Teachers

DAILY SCHEDULE

One difficult job in planning is to arrive at a daily and weekly schedule that will provide adequate time for all of the activities that need to be included. The following description is based on a six-hour day, and when finalized it should be charted in such a manner that teacher or substitute teacher can see at a glance where the group should be and what they should be doing at any given time on any given day.

From Arrival Until 8:00 A.M.

Signing in, giving lunch order, doing any assigned task, independent activity.

8:00 A.M.—11:00 A.M.

This is the main instructional skill-training period. It includes such activities as pegboard work-orders, boltboards, nuts and bolts, sorting, collating, envelope-stuffing, group conveyor-belt or similar activity (at least once weekly), and other types of training activities we have described. In addition, individualized assignments with specialized instruction, drill, and recitation are appropriate. These would be generally in the area of academics, although instruction for a new occupational skill would also take place here.

NOTE: During the months that swimming and bowling are scheduled, these activities would take the place of the work period for such time as they are scheduled. The time for the special teachers of art and music will be scheduled in this period as assigned by the administration. Trips, assemblies, and special events may preempt part of this work period.

11:00 A.M.—11:30 A.M.

Lunch: Allow sufficient time from previous period to get ready.

11:30 A.M.—12:15 P.M.

This is the period for independant activity, grooming activities, and any special individual assignments for various responsibilities.

12:15 P.M.—1:00 P.M.

Physical education: Preferably outdoors when weather permits, indoor games and activities when it does not, one day set aside for folk dancing. (We have found that folk dancing is a good way to end the week on Friday.)

1:00 P.M.—1:30 P.M.

1:30 P.M.—1:55 P.M.

These two periods are in a sense open periods, in that they are reserved for music practice, movies or filmstrips, working on art projects, necessary cleanup or finishing up of work, special events such as birthday celebrations, perhaps a walk on a lovely day—in short, things that need to be done but haven't. They promote flexibility and should be well filled!

1:55 P.M.—2:00 P.M.

Sign out and prepare for dismissal at 2:00 P.M.

DAILY SCHEDULE (School Year) Teacher _____ Grade/Subject _____ School _____					
TIME	**MONDAY**	**TUESDAY**	**WED.**	**THURS.**	**FRIDAY**

WORK RECORD SHEET

An individual work record sheet will vary considerably as a program progresses. Although one continues to record productivity, and skills that have been mastered or are improving, the teacher will continue to add new areas of instruction. When these sheets are analyzed they will in many respects resemble a cumulative record tending to reveal a profile of the trainee's particular abilities and disabilities. A teacher will add pages as necessary. She may decide to have one, two, or several sheets for each month's progress. Categories that have been fully mastered may not appear on later sheets, but may be referred to from an earlier sheet.

A record sheet for "John Brown" may look something like this in the first month:

ASSEMBLING BOLTBOARDS 3, 5, 1, 10, 21, and so on

(Numbers indicating the specific number of the board that has been completed)

DISASSEMBLY OF BOLTBOARDS 2, 12, 11, and so on

(Numbers indicating boards disassembled, but not necessarily assembled by trainee)

SORTING   Boxes 1, 5, 3, 6, and so on

Comments: John is still able to work efficiently with large and medium-size objects and can handle up to six or seven at a time. He is improving rapidly and needs daily practice in sorting.

CONVEYOR BELT   (Use date or a symbol for times he has worked on belt.)

Comments: John works well but needs the simplest assignments. His greatest lack at this time is speed. He works accurately but slowly.

PEGBOARD ASSIGNMENTS

Comments: Is following patterns well. Working on stage three with limited success.

HOUSEKEEPING TASKS

Comments: Works slowly but well. (Teacher might want to record dates he was in charge of cleanup and indicate tasks that need help.)

ACADEMIC SKILLS

Comments: Is working on learning alphabet, tracing, rote counting, and money identification.

SPECIAL ABILITIES

Comments: Unusually good at artwork if given enough time. Socially, is friendly, outgoing. Excellent speech. Good eating habits, but slow.

SPECIAL NEEDS

Comments: Improvement needed in motor and coordinative skills. Needs to try new things. Tends to want to do those things he knows he can do.

LEADERSHIP

Comments: Not really tested as yet. Prefers to follow at this stage.

COLLATING, ENVELOPE-STUFFING, DIVIDERS

Comments: Only beginning. Needs practice.

As many categories should be added as are necessary to indicate the scope of his individualized program and to reveal his progress with it.

VOCATIONAL REHABILITATION COMMISSION

"One of the primary responsibilities of the Division of Vocational Rehabilitation Services is to develop a program of rehabilitation adequate to meet the needs of the State. . . . This involves a determination of the numbers in need, eligible, and the services which these persons need to make them employable. This agency renders a continuing study of the facilities available within the State to meet the needs. On the basis of this information, the overall program of Rehabilitation is planned. These plans, which are properly interpreted to the State Legislature, are the basis for legislative program effecting Rehabilitation, both with respect to appropriations and adequate legal provisions for meeting program needs.

"In the provision of services the agency performs a number of related functions. Some of these functions are as follows:

1. Case findings
2. Determination of eligibility.
3. Individual Written Rehabilitation Program for each client.
4. The provision of Vocational Rehabilitation Services to the disabled. Depending on the need and the number of persons to be served most Counties may have a specialty Rehabilitation Counselor who is involved only with the disability of mental retardation. . . .

William R. Kology, M.A.
Rehabilitation Counselor
Vocational Rehabilitation Commission
Union Co., Elizabeth, N.J. 07201"

Check your telephone book for the office nearest you. Teachers should become acquainted with this office and obtain a supply of applications to keep in the school file. The teacher should initiate the applying and processing of a trainee early in his last year of school. In our experience this department has been most cooperative through the years.

The following booklet and pamphlet contain a complete description of rehabilitation services and other pertinent information:

Summary Edition: The 2nd Half-Century—A Plan for Vocational Rehabilitation to 1975 and Beyond

In Hiring People It's Ability That Counts, Not Disability

Both are available from State of New Jersey, Rehabilitation Commission, Labor and Industry Building, John Fitch Plaza, Room 1210D, Trenton, N.J.

Appendix II

Because of the dearth of printed material useful to the classroom teacher and parent who are training a young retarded adult for work, the authors have been able to list only a few books and articles of possible value.

More extended bibliographies are contained in the sources listed below.

Books and Pamphlets

Carlson, Bernice Wells, and Ginglend, David R. *Play Activities for the Retarded Child.* Nashville: Abingdon, 1961.

————. *Recreation for Retarded Teenagers and Young Adults,* Nashville: Abingdon, 1968.

Ginglend, David R., and Stiles, Winifred E. *Music Activities for Retarded Children,* Nashville: Abingdon, 1965.

DiMichael, Salvatore, ed. *New Vocational Pathways for the Mentally Retarded.* American Personnel and Guidance Association, 1605 New Hampshire Avenue NW, Washington, D.C., 1966.

Perske, Robert. *New Directions for Parents of Persons Who Are Retarded.* Nashville: Abingdon, 1973.

Vandevere, J. Lilian, *Sound Sketches with Rhythm Instruments.* Brooklyn, N.Y.: Carl Van Roy Co., 1958.

Vodola, Thomas. *An Individualized Physical Education for the Handicapped Child. Developmental and Adapted Physical Education. Low Motor Ability Manual.* Project Active, Township of Ocean School District, Dow Avenue, Oakhurst, N.J. 07755.

Articles, Documents, and Reprints

"Activity Programs for the Mentally Retarded." Contributions to the theory and practice of providing vigorous physical activity for the mentally retarded boys and girls. Reprinted from *Journal of Health, Physical Education, Recreation,* April 1966, by the Project on Recreation and Fitness for the Mentally Retarded, American Association for Health, Physical Education and Recreation, 1201 16th Street NW, Washington, D.C., 20036.

Gold, M. W., and Ellis, N. R., eds. "Research on the Vocational Habilitation of the Retarded, the Present, the Future." International

Review of Research in Mental Retardation. New York: Academic Press, 1973.

Luckey, R. E., and Addison, M. R. "The Profoundly Retarded, a New Challenge for Public Education." Education and Training of the Mentally Retarded, 1974.

"Now They Are Grown." Primarily for parents of teen-age and young adult trainable retardates. Documents Section, State of Minnesota, Room 140, Centennial Building, St. Paul, Minn. 55101

"Pilot Study on Swimming for the Severely Mentally Retarded." Ontario Recreation Association, Oshawa, Ontario, Canada.

Smeets, P. M., and Manfredini, D. C. "Skill Centers: A Model Program for Young Severely Retarded Children." Education and Training of the Mentally Retarded, 1973.

"Swimming for the Mentally Retarded." Prepared in cooperation with Richard L. Brown, Director of Water Safety, American National Red Cross. Available through NARC.

"A World of the Right Size," Documents Section, Room 140, Centennial Building, St. Paul, Minn. 53101.

Filmstrip

Vodola, Thomas. *Overview of the Individualized Motor Ability Program.* Project Active, Township of Ocean School District, Dow Avenue, Oakhurst, N.J. 07755.

Extended Bibliographies

Annotated Bibliography: Experimental Education Unit. Child Development and Mental Retardation Center, University of Washington, Seattle, Wash. This project was supported by the Bureau of Education for the Handicapped, U.S. Office of Education, Department of Health, Education and Welfare.

Vocational Education and Work Study Programs. CEC Information on Exceptional Children, 1499 Jefferson Davis Highway, Suite 900, Arlington, Va. 22202.

Specialized bibliographies may be obtained from the following sources:

Association for the Help of Retarded Citizens, New City Chapter, 200 Park Avenue S., New York, N.Y. 10003.

Joseph P. Kennedy, Jr. Foundation, Suite 402, 1411 K. Street NW, Washington, D.C.

National Association for Retarded Citizens. 2709 Avenue E East, P. O. Box 6109, Arlington, Tex. 76011.

U.S. Department of Health, Education and Welfare, Superintendant of Documents, Washington, D.C.

Cooperative Publication Association. P. O. Box 179, St. Louis, Mo. 63166.

Index

Index

Sorting and matching, 39-42
Spring musical programs, 104
Stapling, 51
Sticks on cards, 52
Stockings, paper, 108
Subtraction, 71
Superintendent, role of, 135
Swimming, 95

Table, setting, 62-63
Teachers, types of, 135
Teams, making of, 87-88
Teen-age art festival, 111
Time schedule, daily, 23, 149
Toilet accidents, 122
Toothbrushing, 120
Transfer of learning, 37
Transportation, teaching, 141

Trips, 125-28
TV in classroom, 33

Vocational Rehabilitation Commission, 137, 152

Wall hangings, 113
Work
at home, 143
part-time, 143
teaching the concept of, 17-19
Work record sheets, 61, 150
Work sheets, 25
Workshops, sheltered, 16, 36
Wreaths, paper, 108
Writing, how to teach, 67, 70